PHILOSOPHICAL THINKING IN EDUCATIONAL PRACTICE

PHILOSOPHICAL THINKING IN EDUCATIONAL PRACTICE

Robert D. Heslep

Westport, Connecticut
London

Library of Congress Cataloging-in-Publication Data

Heslep, Robert D.
  Philosophical thinking in educational practice / Robert D. Heslep.
      p.   cm.
  Includes bibliographical references (p.) and index.
  ISBN 0–275–95495–1 (alk. paper). — ISBN 0–275–95496–X (pbk : alk.
paper)
    1. Education—Philosophy. 2. Education—Aims and objectives.
  I. Title.
  LB885.H45P48 1997
  370′.1—dc21   96–53935

British Library Cataloguing in Publication Data is available.

Library of Congress Catalog Card Number: 96–53935
ISBN: 0–275–95495–1
      0–275–95496–X (pbk.)

First published in 1997

Praeger Publishers, 88 Post Road West, Westport, CT 06881
An imprint of Greenwood Publishing Group, Inc.

Printed in the United States of America

The paper used in this book complies with the
Permanent Paper Standard issued by the National
Information Standards Organization (Z39.48–1984).

10 9 8 7 6 5 4 3 2 1

Contents

Preface

This text differs from many others that address the philosophy of education. It does not focus on the history of educational philosophy even though it recognizes how rich and extensive that history is. It does not systematically follow the branches of philosophy, often taken to be metaphysics, ethics, epistemology, and logic. It does not center around "schools" of educational philosophy, neither the hoary ones of Idealism, Realism, Pragmatism, Existentialism, and Phenomenology nor the trendy ones of Critical Theory, Post-Structuralism, Post-Modernism, and Gender Philosophy. Finally, it has little concern with bodies of doctrine called "philosophies of education," for instance, Perennialism, Essentialism, Progressivism, and Democratic Education.

Instead of concentrating on any of these matters, this text presents educational philosophy mainly as a variety of philosophical thinking, or thought, which includes both process and content or method and principles. More specifically, the text takes such intellectual activity chiefly to be the quest for a certain kind of understanding, the quest that the ancient Greeks called "the love of wisdom." But this book does not present the philosophy of education just for its own sake. Rather, it largely and ultimately attempts to show the practical value of such philosophy.

A thesis of this book is that teachers, administrators, and other educational practitioners are committed to a fundamental understanding of their goals and the actions by which they attempt to attain them. Such understanding is practical wisdom. While philosophical thought aims at general and abstract wisdom, it is applicable to practical affairs. When educators integrate philosophical methods and ideas into their thinking, they engage in practical reason; they are able to obtain a basic understanding of their goals and actions. While a philosophical orientation to educational practice might include the commonsensical considerations of educators, it goes beyond these considerations in that it checks the justifiability of these received beliefs. While this orientation does include critical thinking, it is not just critical thinking for the reason that the former, but not the latter, necessarily aims at choices and decisions. While a philosophical approach to educational practice is not scientific, it does not purport to compete with or supplant scientific research on education; indeed, it leaves to science the field of theoretical knowledge obtained through empirical methods.

An additional thesis of this text is that the quest for philosophical understanding is a kind of questioning. Since ancient times, philosophers have been famous for posing questions and looking for answers to them. Their inquiry has included perennial as well as topical questions and has been systematic at times and unsystematic at others, explicit at times and implicit at others. Philosophers, thus, have tended to agree that their thinking begins in wonder, doubt, puzzlement, or some other mode of questioning. So, in maintaining that philosophical thinking may be of value to educational practitioners, I simply mean that they will be able to gain a deep understanding of their goals and actions if they raise questions about those goals and actions so as to find logically firm ground for having or rejecting them. This ground, however, does not have to be absolutely firm. A foundation does not have to be for all times and all places in order to be stable.

Another thesis is that there are general and abstract ideas about education that arguably are acceptable to both philosophers and educators and that can serve the educators as principles for questioning their goals and actions. One of these ideas is that educational practitioners, students, parents, and other interested persons ultimately are moral agents, that is, interpersonal, knowledgeable, and free doers of things. Another idea is that moral agency entails certain values, rights, duties, and virtues related to being interpersonal, knowledgeable, and free. A further idea is that educators, students, parents, and others interested in education have special values, rights, duties, and virtues shaped by the specific aspects of their respective situations as moral agents. Accordingly, in saying that these ideas can serve educators as principles for questioning their goals and actions, I intend that teachers, administrators, and others will raise questions about their practice of education as it pertains to the features and norms of moral agency. For instance, is a given society's notion of education compatible with the purposiveness and deliberativeness of moral agents? Is compulsory education consistent with the freedom of moral agents? Is the tracking of students compatible with the equality of moral agents? If an official educational policy violates the norms of moral agency, should it be obeyed?

Finally, this volume submits that a discussion of cases of educational practice will be especially useful in helping prospective and occurrent educators to learn to seek a profound understanding of their goals and actions. Even though a discussion of general educational issues certainly can help students learn about general aspects of particular educational situations, it will not provide students with insights into posing questions about the particularities inherent in practical educational situations. The discussion of questions bearing on cases enables students to deal with particulars. Accordingly, the bulk of this volume will consist of case analysis. The cases to be examined will be realistic but fictional. They are in no way intended to depict real persons, schools, or events.

The approach to the study of educational philosophy set forth here plainly gives greater attention to the moral aspects of educational practice than it does to its logical, metaphysical, or epistemological dimensions. This does not mean, however, that the approach is unduly weighted toward moral considerations. By its very concept, educational practice is a species of moral action. Hence, it would be unjustifiable to play down or ignore the moral features of such practice. Moreover, thinking about the goals and actions of educational practice invariably raises normative questions but typically considers logical, metaphysical, or epistemological ones only as they arise in connection with normative ones. It seems appropriate, therefore, to take up the logical, metaphysical, and epistemological features of educational practice only as they are situated within the framework of moral agency. This text attempts to consider these features in this way. Thus, it proposes that the study of educational philosophy will enable students to become not philosophers but educators disposed to attain practical wisdom.

1

The Study of Educational Philosophy: Part One

Many persons wanting to acquire competence as school teachers or administrators study the philosophy of education. Why, however, should any educational practitioner be versed in this field?

The standard argument against the study of educational philosophy centers on the connection between theory and practice. Philosophy of any type is theoretical. It deals, in a purely intellectual way, with general and abstract matters without necessarily influencing the world of action. By contrast, teaching, school administration, and all other educational activities are practical. They necessarily affect action; more specifically, they set purposes for action and set courses of action in particular and concrete situations. How could prospective or actual educational practitioners benefit, then, from the study of the philosophy of education? While the examination of various philosophical ideas about education might have general importance for any educational context, it has no special significance for the particular situations with which individual practitioners must deal. While learning about the different methods that philosophers employ in theorizing about education might prove intellectually interesting, it will not prepare future or present practitioners specifically for formulating goals and making decisions. Besides, student educators have sufficient access to ideas for conceiving purposes and to skills for deciding on actions. The ideas are those of professional common sense, which include the familiar findings of applied educational research. The skills are those of practical reasoning.

This argument cannot be ignored. Not only does it logically compel us and anyone else concerned with the education of educators to consider whether or not the study of educational philosophy should be a part of this education, but it also lies at the backs of the minds, if not on the tips of the tongues, of most would-be and occurrent practitioners taking classes in the subject. Nevertheless, the argument should not be readily viewed as insuperable. Perhaps there is some way that educational philosophy can be practically relevant. Perhaps professional common sense is not sufficient for guiding educational choices. Perhaps practical reasoning, at least as it is popularly understood, is not sufficient for setting goals and deciding on actions. Indeed, it might be that the study of educational philosophy can serve a vital need of educators.

I invite the reader to consider a five-step argument supporting this possibility. This chapter contains the initial two steps. The first step identifies the major need that can be met by the study of educational philosophy. That need bears on the point that educational practitioners are logically committed to a questioning of their purposes and decisions. The second step examines the traditional approaches to studying educational philosophy. This critique will hold that none of these approaches is likely to prepare educators to satisfy the need of concern.

THE EDUCATOR AS RATIONAL AGENT

There are practitioners in various fields, for instance, medicine, law, religion, engineering, the military, nursing, and education. Fields with practitioners are widely called *professions.* Any profession, even if it is less than a model of the concept, shares certain characteristics with all others (Etzioni, 1969). It performs a definite public function; it involves skills and knowledge derived from experience as well as technical skills and special knowledge grounded on theory; and its practitioners perform its public function by employing the profession's skills and applying its knowledge. Thus, in medicine the public function is to provide health care; the chemical and biological sciences constitute the bulk of the theoretical foundation of medical research; and physicians look after the public's health needs by using their medical skills and knowledge. In education, the public function is to enable learning; the theoretical basis of professional knowledge consists of the humanities and the natural and social sciences; and teachers and school administrators are expected to have expertise in pedagogy and in organizing faculty and acquiring material resources for educational ends.

Some practitioners perform their professional function by making things, as in the case of construction engineers who make bridges and dams. Others perform their professional function by providing services, as in the case of accountants who analyze the financial records of business institutions. Educators usually perform services rather than produce things. But whether practitioners make things or provide services, they are agents, that is, people who engage in action or do things. They are not, however, blind agents; they choose the particular ends their actions are to attain. Moreover, they are deliberative; they weigh alternative courses of action for attaining their ends and decide which actions are right. Thus, physicians decide on therapies to remedy the particular conditions of given patients; architects decide on specific materials for constructing particular buildings; and teachers decide on particular strategies for getting different students to learn certain facts, skills, or attitudes.

According to the ordinary conception of the matter, practitioners are neither capricious nor arbitrary in picking their particular goals. Instead, they are judgmental; that is, they choose goals that they deem to be worthy. Their judgments rest, explicitly or implicitly, on relevant facts and appropriate professional norms. When making decisions, practitioners supposedly ground them, in view of their purposes, on available technical skills and research and on the common sense that has developed within their individual professions. People who profess to be practitioners but who make decisions by impulse, superstition, coin flips, or other similiar ways are unprofessional and popularly regarded as quacks. Practitioners, in brief, select only goals and actions that they can justify, that is, for which they can offer sufficiently good reasons.

In being committed to justifiable goals and actions, practitioners are committed also to questioning. They must ask not only such questions as, "Why should this end be pursued?" and "Why is this action right?", but they must ask also such questions as, "Are these good reasons?" and "Does this decision logically follow from these reasons?" In asking if reasons are good, one seeks to know if they are clear in meaning, self-consistent, relevant, and consistent with each other. In asking if judgments or decisions logically follow from stated reasons, one seeks to know if they violate the principles and rules of inference, whether deductive, inductive, or some other kind. Because practitioners want justifiable goals and actions, they are prepared to question their judgments, decisions, and all supporting reasons fully. This means they may wonder about even the major principles of their profession, including its public function, the theoretical basis of its research, and its store of common sense.

In this century, there have been scattered instances of wide-range questioning within professions. During recent decades, some physicians have challenged the traditional notion that their professional function is mainly to treat or prevent disease; they have proposed that the function should focus instead on the promotion of health. In-house criticisms of the American legal profession have been popular lately, especially those directed at its adversarial approach to justice. Since the end of the nineteenth century, members of the education profession have posed critical questions. What should be the function of the public school? What should be the responsibility of teachers? Should social needs or student interests receive priority? Should educational research be modeled strictly after scientific research?

At times, insider questions about the education profession, as well as other kinds of questions, have been less than disinterested searches for answers. Some have been self-serving, highly emotional, and narrowly political. Recent instances of such questions appear in the disputes over standardized testing, merit pay, site-based management, outcome-based education, sex education, multicultural education, moral education, and religious instruction. There is, however, no anomaly here, for spoken questions have different functions. While they may serve as signs of quests for information or understanding, they may serve too as polite commands, expressions of helplessness, expressions of doubt, indirect statements of belief, and in other ways. When educators are true to the concept of a practitioner, they engage in questioning mainly in order to obtain information or understanding. Their questioning with other motives must be secondary.

So, in the respect that teachers, school administrators, and other educators are practitioners, they need to be prepared to undertake extensive questioning of the goals and actions they consider. To be sure, the principles of their profession can help them in this questioning. Social science research can provide them with knowledge about which actions are likely to be effective in attaining which goals. Professional common sense can furnish them with insights into what should and should not be done in different kinds of circumstances. The public function of the profession establishes an overarching aim with respect to which goals are to be formulated and which courses of action are to be conceived. These principles, however, are not beyond question. It is not evident that the immense variety of differences among actual educational situations are amenable to the uniformities presumed by scientific research. It is not apparent that obedience of the law, which is a tenet of the common sense of educators, should be blind. Also, it is not obvious that past experience, which is another article of their common sense, is invariably applicable to present or future situations. Finally, it is not clear what the public function of the education profession is. Where does its function leave off and that of, for instance, the family, the community, the mass media, or business begin? Accordingly, becoming versed in the common sense and function of the educational profession is not a sufficient preparation for its members to question their goals and actions as much as they might have to.

It appears, then, that educators cannot gain this preparation unless they are able to question the foundations of their profession and other matters beyond it that are related to their goals and actions. Let us now consider whether or not the established paths in the study of educational philosophy are likely to develop this ability in students.

ESTABLISHED APPROACHES TO STUDYING EDUCATIONAL PHILOSOPHY

According to the ancient biographer, Diogenes Laertius (1925), the term *philosophy* was coined by Pythagoras, the Greek philosopher and mathematician. The term means the love of, or the affinity for, wisdom or, more specifically, wisdom about general and abstract matters. Before Pythagoras, people devoted to wisdom were called wise men rather than philosophers. But because Pythagoras held that only God should be called wise, he invented *philosophy* as a term for referring to the human effort to obtain wisdom.

It should not be thought, however, that human interest in wisdom originated with Greek intellectuals, whether they were known as wise men or as philosophers. That interest certainly was present in Greek religion, which predates Greek philosophy. Thus, Athena was the goddess of practical wisdom among other things. Apollo made known to human beings, through oracles and prophets, his knowledge of the future and the mind of Zeus, the head god. Moreover, there were

African and Middle Eastern strands in the "wisdom tradition" that were independent of and possibly influential to the Greeks (Meyer, 1992, p. 8). In Egypt, there was a line of sages beginning some time in the third millenium B.C. That line included Amenemhat, Amenemope, Ptahhotep, and others. Such intellectuals were present also in Babylonia and may have been present in Canaan before it was conquered by the Hebrews. The Old Testament, which mentions female as well as male figures of wisdom (*II Sam.* xx, 16–22), is renowned for its wisdom books, *Proverbs*, *Job*, and *Ecclesiastes*. In addition, there was a wisdom tradition in ancient India that developed independently of Greece.

In these various cultures, there were collectively three kinds of wisdom. There was the divine word, which was spoken by oracles (for instance, the one at the Greek city of Delphi) or by prophets (such as the Persian Zarathustra) or was written (as in the Indian *Vedas*). Moreover, there was the interpretation of the divine word, as in the *Brahmanas*, which are that part of the *Vedas* that includes commentary on the *Vedas*'s sacred texts. Lastly, there were counsel, truth, and understanding conceived strictly through human intelligence. This wisdom sometimes took the form of proverbs or expressions of insights into worldly affairs. Such insights we might call "practical wisdom." The third kind of wisdom also took the form of statements of truth and understanding about general and abstract matters, such as human values, the source of knowledge, the meaning of life, and the nature of things. It is this latter type of wisdom in which classical Greek philosophers were interested and in which philosophers since them have been interested. Hence, it is traditionally called "philosophical wisdom."

That a person is a philosopher does not mean that he or she is a sage. While the love of wisdom means that one seeks wisdom, it does not ensure that one obtains wisdom. Thus, Socrates (470?–399 B.C.), the quintessential philosopher, held that the only thing he knew was that he knew not. For Plato (427–347 B.C.), Socrates' most famous pupil, the philosopher was a person who sought knowledge of forms, or ideals, through a dialectical method. For Aristotle (384–322 B.C.), Plato's most famous pupil, the possession of wisdom was an intellectual excellence, whereas philosophy was not for the reason that it was a search for, rather than the possession of, wisdom. It is arguable, therefore, that the "quest of philosophers" for wisdom is as distinctive of themselves as is the wisdom that they attain. So, if the study of educational philosophy is to be of practical value, it will be so because of one or both of these factors: the general and abstract wisdom that students might learn and some feature of the philosophic search for that wisdom, which students might acquire as a skill.

The Wisdom of Educational Philosophy

Because the accumulated wisdom of philosophy has been developed by innumerable thinkers from diverse cultures for a period of 4,000 years and more, it is very extensive, complex, and often at odds with itself. This point holds also for what philosophy has to say about education. Not surprisingly, then, it is quite difficult to teach philosophy's ideas about the subject. In the United States and elsewhere, several broad approaches to teaching these ideas have been employed so as to organize the study of the subject.

One way may be described as doctrinal. Rather than dwelling on the ideas that underlie a particular philosopher's position on education, this orientation centers around beliefs about education that have been distilled from the mass of educational philosophy. Widely recognized examples of educational doctrines are Perennialism, Essentialism, and Progressivism. The tenets learned by students need not be formally established. Thus, while some students might learn the tenets of Democratic Education only, others might learn the various bodies of belief that they implicitly hold already. Regardless of the diversity of doctrines studied, however, this orientation has practical worth in that it suggests practical educational beliefs to would-be practitioners and encourages teachers and administrators to articulate the educational beliefs they already have.

While this route to the study of educational philosophy was rather popular before World War II, it also was liable to extensive criticisms (Broudy, 1979). A couple of these criticisms are pertinent to our inquiry. Because students, according to this approach, are to learn educational beliefs separated from their respective underlying philosophical ideas, they will not learn to justify their educational principles, let alone question the ideas supporting them. The other pertinent criticism concerns the fact that opposing beliefs about educational practice might be compatible with the same educational principles. For instance, one teacher might believe that students should do their class work individually whereas another might believe that they should work in groups. Both beliefs, however, are compatible with tenets of Democratic Education, such as equal educational opportunity, respect for others, and acceptance of responsibility. But because students, according to the doctrinal orientation, are to use educational principles to determine the practical guidelines that they are to follow, they will not be able to know which of the guidelines to follow if their educational principles allow opposing guidelines. They might be in a position to know this if they were prepared to question their principles, seeking clarification of them by examining their underlying ideas. By the doctrinal orientation, however, students are not to be concerned with underlying ideas.

Another approach to teaching philosophical wisdom about education has been to organize that wisdom according to "schools" of philosophy (National Society for the Study of Education, 1942; 1955). According to this approach, philosophical wisdom consists of the answers that philosophers have given to their perennial questions, frequently called "philosophical issues." Moreover, these questions address certain broad topics, most notably existence, ethical standards, and knowledge. Finally, the answers that philosophers have given to questions related to each of these topics form the bases of schools of philosophy. One traditional classification of philosophical schools consists of Progressivism, Essentialism, and Perennialism (Brameld, 1955), which should not be confused with the groupings of educational doctrines that go by the same names. Another familiar scheme consists of Realism, Idealism, Pragmatism, and Existentialism (Morris, 1961).

Realists hold that reality is objective and physical; that values, rights, and duties are natural (classical Realism) or just personal or cultural preferences (modern Realism); and that knowledge of reality must come through empirical means, especially the scientific method. Idealists, to cite only one more example, typically maintain that reality is objective but nonphysical, that basic norms are Ideals independent of human influence, and that knowledge of reality is to be had through pure reason. More recent identifications of philosophical schools are Phenomenology, Philosophical Analysis, Postmodernism, and what for convenience may be called "Genderism" (Ozmon and Craver, 1995; Noddings, 1995). The last school contains philosophical responses classified according to gender distinctions, for instance, feminine and masculine theories of existence, feminine and masculine ethics, and feminine and masculine theories of knowledge.

Each philosophical school supposedly has general implications for education. Thus, for modern Realism, the purpose of education is to prepare students, according to their abilities, to understand and live within the boundaries of nature and society; the curriculum is to emphasize science and technology; and teaching and administration are to be based on scientific research. For Idealism, the purpose of education is to develop within students, according to their respective limits, moral ideals and the ability to reason about nonphysical as well as physical matters; the curriculum is to focus on classical works; and teaching and administration are to be arts informed by a cognizance and appreciation of ideals as well as by experience. For Existentialism, the purpose of education is to help students become autonomous beings, that is, beings capable of giving their respective lives meaning through their individual choices. The curriculum is to consist of, in addition to academic subjects, the development of student interests, the exploration of alternative ways of life, and the acquisition of competence in judgment and deliberation. Teaching is to facilitate, not control, learning while administration is to be open and participatory. For Genderism, the purpose of education is to help students to become knowledgable and respectful of the various gender outlooks on the world and to develop a character composed of the desirable features of either or both of the two genders.

It is the alleged general educational implications of the various schools of philosophy that presumably make it possible for the study of educational philosophy to be important for practitioners. Not only can students of the subject learn about the philosophical schools' respective implications for education in general, but they can learn also how these implications might apply to the classroom and other arenas of educational practice. Indeed, textbooks employing the schools approach sometimes have made special efforts to relate these implications to specific practices of teachers and administrators (Morris, 1961).

Nevertheless, the schools orientation is subject to objections. This approach does not explain why it classifies philosophical systems according to their responses to some philosophical issues but not to others. For instance, it does not tell why those systems are to be categorized according to their answers to questions about reality and norms but not about their subject matters and principles. Not explaining why one classificatory schema is used rather than another, the schools approach does not enable students to understand if all schemata are equally defensible. Moreover, this orientation does not prepare students to critique the different philosophical schools included in a given schema; it simply explains to the students what the features of the various schools are. Hence, it does not furnish students with a means for rationally choosing among the various philosophical schools and their implied educational principles. Finally, this approach, like the doctrinal one, does not prepare students to understand how to weigh against one another diverse educational practices compatible with the same educational principles.

The last approach to learning the wisdom of educational philosophy that we will consider is to study the educational theories of individual philosophers (Brumbaugh and Lawrence, 1963; Reed and Johnson, 1996). The theories studied are to be diverse as well as manageable in number. They might include those of past philosophers, for example, Jean Jacques Rousseau (French, 1712–1978), Johann Friedrich Herbart (German, 1776–1841), Herbert Spencer (English, 1820–1903), John Dewey (American, 1859–1952), and Alfred North Whitehead (English, 1861–1947). They also might include theories by contemporary philosophers, such as the Americans Israel Scheffler and Maxine Greene. Students are not to be especially concerned with identifying the respective strengths and weaknesses of the theories studied. Rather, they are to compare and contrast the theories so as to regard them as alternative guides to educational practice. They thereby will have a repertoire of theories from which to choose for practical guidance. Which theory a practitioner is to follow is left to his or her discretion. Whether or not a practitioner faithfully follows a chosen theory is left to his or her judgment.

Unfortunately, this orientation also suffers defects. Because it does not provide students with a means for assessing the various philosopical bases of given educational theories, it does not encourage them to question those theories thoroughly. Also, because it does not furnish students with a method for applying the theories, it does not incline them to question the faithfulness of their practices to their chosen theories.

Features of Philosophical Thinking

Having found serious deficiencies in the customary proposals for studying philosophical wisdom about education, we now will consider whether or not any of the usual proposals for studying the features of philosophical thinking will be satisfactory. While there are educational philosophers who hold that educators should acquire skills involved in philosophical thinking, there are differences among them on what skills are to be learned and to what end they are to be learned.

One position is that teachers and administrators should have skills for making proper inferences, clarifying meanings, forming concepts, explaining, and justifying (Hullfish and Smith, 1963; Ennis, 1969). Having these abilities will help teachers know how to think and talk logically in the classroom. It also will help teachers to pass these skills on to their students in an effort to make them reflective citizens. In addition, possession of such skills will help administrators to understand and appreciate the teacher's task and thus to maintain a school climate that will foster that task. A related position is that educational practitioners should have the skills, dispositions, and appreciations of critical thinking (Siegel, 1988). From this viewpoint, critical thinking is a matter of rationality, or believing and acting on the basis of reasons; it is seeking reasons on which to ground judgments and actions. As critical thinkers, therefore, teachers and administrators are committed to rationality as a goal and content of education, but they are committed to it also as an educational ideal, which can be used to weigh competing methods, policies, and practices (Siegel, 1988, pp. 32–33, 46). In other words, when educators face alternatives, they must pursue those that more closely approximate rationality, that is, those that rest on better reasons.

Having maintained already that educators are rational agents, we can only agree that such practitioners should be rational, whether in the sense of logical, reflective, or critical. To be sure, philosophy is not unique in its concern with rationality. All intellectual disciplines intend for their inquiries to be rational, and all practical fields emphasize the importance of basing judgments and decisions on reasons. Nevertheless, philosophy, which seeks wisdom strictly through reason, has been traditionally the discipline that has been especially interested in rationality as a subject of investigation. The other disciplines have been concerned with it as it applies specifically to their respective inquiries, and the various fields of practice have dealt with it as it specifically applies to them. Educational philosophy, consequently, is a highly appropriate area for students to gain skills, dispositions, and appreciations of rationality. If students learn these dimensions of rationality as they relate specifically to the practice of teaching and administration, students presumably will find their study of educational philosophy important for their professional work.

Yet, even though we must acknowledge that reason is integral to the practice of education, we must wonder if a concentration on reasoning is worthwhile. More specifically, we have to wonder if such a concentration misrepresents reasoning in educational practice or ignores something vital to such practice. Rationality, we are told, is *an* ideal of education; it is *a* standard against which competing methods, policies, and practices must be weighed. Supposedly, then, rationality is not the only ideal of education. We are not told, however, what the other ideals are. Not knowing what they are, we do not know how they relate to rationality. Are they equal, inferior, or superior to it? Are they independent of it? Are they mutually dependent with rationality? Thus, a focus upon rationality misrepresents educational practice if the latter involves reasoning mainly in connection with other ideals. Also, such a focus fails to help aspiring and actual educators learn about the other ideal elements involved in education.

Another position concerned with philosophical thinking is notably different from the ones we have just examined. Instead of holding that educators should become proficient in only some of the features of philosophical thinking, this view advocates that they should master all of its features and consequently become capable of philosophizing (Simpson and Jackson, 1984). According to this view, then, educators should learn to engage in what the view regards as the three modes of philosophical activity: analysis, judgment, and synopsis. As an analytic thinker, the philosophical educator will clarify meanings and critique arguments in educational discourse. As a normative thinker, the philosophical educator will look for sound reasons for choosing goals and deciding upon actions. As a synoptic thinker, the philosophical educator will strive to see the world of education in its totality.

There is no question that this way offers the education student much that will be of practical value. Teachers and administrators do need to be clear and logical in their communications with students and among themselves. They do need to identify sound reasons for their choices and decisions. And so as not to confuse their respective sectors of education with the whole of it, they do need to understand how their individual areas fit with all others. Nevertheless, one suspects that this approach to studying the philosophy of education expects more of the student than is feasible. It is one thing for educators to be analytical, thoughtful in judgment, and inclined to relate matters to one another. It is quite another for them to be philosophers. Since the time of ancient Greece, it has been customary to distinguish philosophical reason from practical reason. Philosophical reason seeks general and abstract wisdom (in transliteration, the Greek for such wisdom is *sophia*). Practical reason seeks wisdom that is specific and relates to the concrete world (*phronesis*). Plato maintained that it was the philosopher's duty to apply his or her discovered wisdom to the practical world, and Aristotle allowed that the practical person may use philosophical wisdom as basic principles of judgments and decisions. Neither of them held, however, that educators or other practical people become philosophers simply by making use of philosophical skills. To become philosophers, educators must learn to undertake the quest for general and abstract wisdom. It is dubious, however, that they can learn to do this in a brief study of educational philosophy.

CONCLUSION

To answer the question of why prospective or occurrent educators should study educational philosophy, we have undertaken an inquiry to see if learning about such philosophy might satisfy a major need of educational practitioners. In the first phase of the inquiry, we argued that educators logically need to understand their purposes and decisions thoroughly. In the second phase, we concluded that none of the traditional approaches to studying educational philosophy that we reviewed shows promise of preparing educators to understand their purposes and decisions fully. If, therefore, learning about educational philosophy is likely to prepare educators in this respect, that learning will have to be by some orientation not yet examined. In the next chapter, the argument that we are following will specify a way to make practically valuable the study of educational philosophy by educators.

2

The Study of Educational Philosophy: Part Two

We have been considering whether or not there is a way to study educational philosophy that will give the subject practical importance. Thinking that that issue can be settled in the affirmative, I proposed an argument consisting of five steps, two of which we already have taken. In its first step, the argument contended that educators have a need to question their purposes and decisions; in the second step, it held that the traditional approaches to studying educational philosophy do not adequately help educators meet that need. We now will proceed with the remaining three steps. To that end, I shall try to show that philosophy of any kind seeks understanding mainly through a kind of questioning, that educational practitioners are moral agents in a special setting, and that the study of educational philosophy as the indicated kind of questioning will be applicable to the world of educational practice if the study gives extensive attention to cases involving educators. As far as I can tell, these points do not receive due recognition in any of the customary orientations we examined in the previous chapter.

PHILOSOPHIZING AS QUESTIONING

As practitioners, we have argued, educators logically need to raise basic questions about their goals and actions, even about the principles of their profession. If, therefore, the study of educational philosophy can enable them to pose such questions, it will be of practical importance for them. Also, if the study of educational philosophy is to help educators ask basic questions about their work, it will have to view the subject as especially concerned with questioning. Let us consider, then, whether or not it makes sense to interpret educational philosophy in this regard.

When reviewing the traditional routes to studying educational philosophy, we stated that two of them centered around features of philosophical thinking. One of them focused on what it recognized to be only some of these features, namely, drawing inferences, clarifying meanings, explaining, and justifying. The other emphasized what it took to be the whole spectrum of philosophizing: analysis, judgment, and synopsis. However, neither of these orientations attempted to relate, in a serious way, the features that it emphasized to questioning. Moreover, neither of them declared whether or not questioning is a central trait of philosophical thinking.

Beginning no later than Socrates, who was famous for engaging in dialogues through questioning, Greek thinkers took the quest for philosophical understanding to be a consideration of questions, implicitly or explicitly posed. More specifically, they took this quest to be the recognition of lacks of understanding about general and abstract matters and the attempt to remedy those lacks. As Aristotle (1961, p. 13) remarked in his book *The Metaphysics,* "It is owing to their wonder that men both now begin and at first began to philosophize." Subsequent philosophers have developed various conceptions of their field, but they historically have allowed that philosophy typically involves wondering, doubting, puzzling, or some other variety of questioning. The scholastic method of medieval European philosophy explicitly involved a systematic examination of questions (McKeon, 1957). While modern Western philosophers rarely have engaged in a systematic discussion of questions, they often have posed them, as when Martin Heidegger (1949; German, 1889–1976) asked, "Why is there any Being at all—why not far rather Nothing?"; and as when the American John R. Searle (1995) asked how social facts are connected with mental and physical ones. Moreover, these philosophers commonly have acknowledged the connection between questioning and philosophizing, which Rene Descartes (1955; French, 1596–1650) regarded as resolving doubts through a method of analysis and synthesis and which John

Dewey (1938; American, 1859–1952) conceived as inquiry into highly general and abstract problems.

Because the answers that philosophers have given to questions typically depend on the principles and methods they respectively have held and used, their answers often do not settle questions once and for all. Questions answered by a philosopher with one set of principles and one kind of method usually get recurrently asked and answered by philosophers with other sets of principles and other kinds of methods. Many questions addressed by philosophers, therefore, are traditional, for instance: What is truth? What can be known? What is real? Are human beings free? Are values objective? The stock questions of philosophy are what is sometimes meant by "philosophical issues."

Even though philosophers have differed in the specific methods they have employed in examining questions (McKeon, 1951), they have agreed that their methods must be rational. More specifically, the methods must follow, for instance, the principles of identity, noncontradiction, and justifiability, as well as the rules of inference. Thus, philosophers have assumed that the questions they investigate are what they are and not something else. They have tried to avoid contradictions in their respective answers, and they have tried to give good reasons for their answers. Being committed to rationality, philosophical inquiry differs from any form of theology that accepts answers based on nothing more than faith; from rhetoric, which seeks acceptance of answers mainly through linguistic devices; from tradition, which maintains that answers must conform to what is customary; and from the exercise of power, which gets answers accepted through institutional control, intimidation, or threat.

Despite the care with which philosophers have investigated questions, they frequently have found that their respective answers, even while initially seeming to be justified, have suggested additional questions. Thus, when the ancient Greek Democritus resolved the issue of the basic constituents of existence by claiming that they are indivisible bits of physical matter, he faced the further question of how it is that there are differences between mind and body. Why one question suggests another is explainable partly by logic and partly by experience. That is, some answers suggest other questions in that they logically presuppose them; some answers suggest other questions because of what our experience tells us about those answers. If, for instance, the answer to the question "What is a line?" is "A series of points," that answer logically presupposes the question of what is a point. If the answer to the question "Is God all knowing, good, and powerful?" is "Yes," that answer raises the question of why God allows all the evil that one has experienced. Philosophers, then, do not count an answer as justified until all questions originated by that answer have been justifiably answered. To justify their answers to those questions, philosophers ultimately have to offer fundamental ideas. It is by justifying their answers to their questions that philosophers fill in the gaps in their understanding and gain wisdom (Macmillan and Garrison, 1988; Heslep, 1991).

Because philosophical thinking has to overcome difficulties in thought and language in order to answer its questions, it frequently is analytic, looking for problems in logic and meaning. Moreover, because such thinking characteristically addresses ethical, political, and aesthetic issues, it often is concerned with ethical, political, and aesthetic norms and judgments involving those norms. In addition, because of the complexity and profundity of its questioning, philosophical thinking must be circumspect, flexible, insightful, and alert to connections. Hence, it lends itself to being synoptic.

Two other qualities of philosophical mindedness follow from its concern with questioning. In dealing with their chains and clusters of questions, philosophers have tended to move from an examination of the particular to the specific, from the specific to the general, and from the concrete to the less tangible, from the less tangible to the abstract. When discussing the particular and concrete, philosophers typically have treated them as instances of the general and the abstract or as starting points for comprehending the latter. Accordingly, the questions raised by philosophers characteristically have been general and abstract; the wisdom that they have obtained has also been general and abstract.

In its broadest meaning, common sense is the opinions about life that human beings tend to hold and by which they tend to have satisfactory lives. Commonsense decisions typically rely upon experience, interest, law, custom, and other elements closely related to the practical world. While commonsense lacks intellectuality, it shares in some of the qualities associated with philosophical thinking. It too may be given, albeit not in a systematic or self-conscious way, to questioning and thus may be reflective, inquisitive, and insightful. Nevertheless, it crucially differs from philosophical thinking in that its questions are about the particular and concrete, the specific and less tangible, but not the general and abstract. Indeed, because common sense focuses on particular and concrete matters, it is a source of expertise on them. The notorious ignorance of philosophers about the "real" world has existed at least since the days of the ancient Greek thinker Thales, who reputedly fell into a manure pile while he was gazing one evening at the heavens.

Philosophy, however, is not the only variety of intellect that seeks to resolve, through rational methods, puzzlements about general and abstract matters. Mathematics and science also have this characteristic although they differ from philosophy. The former ways of thinking historically were sometimes intertwined with the philosophical, but in the modern era, they have separated from it. With the advent of non-Euclidean geometry, in the nineteenth century, pure mathematics ceased to be concerned with the relations of its ideas to the rest of the world; it began to confine its questions to the operations that may be performed, according to certain principles and rules, with nonreferential symbols (Barker, 1964). Thus, even though philosophers sometimes puzzle over the principles and methods employed in mathematics and occasionally attempt to determine its logical foundations, they do not raise questions primarily about the general and abstract matters investigated by modern mathematics.

Beginning with physics and chemistry in the seventeenth and eighteenth centuries and continuing with the biological and social sciences in the nineteenth and twentieth centuries, science has established itself as the authoritative field of general and abstract empirical knowledge about specific aspects of the physical, social, and psychical world (Mason, 1962). So, even though modern philosophy might inquire into the foundations of science and ask questions about physical, social, and psychical existence in general, it does not pretend to investigate specific facets of existence of these sorts, and it certainly does not rely mainly on empirical methods. Metaphysics, epistemology, and logic are supplements to, not rivals of, mathematics and science.

EDUCATORS AS MORAL AGENTS

While we have not tried exhaustively to defend the position that questioning is *a*, perhaps *the*, central feature of philosophizing, we have endeavored to make it at least plausible. Yet, even if we had shown beyond any possible dispute that philosophical mindedness at its core is a matter of questioning, we would not have thereby shown much about how to lend practical worth to the study of educational philosophy. The reason why not is plain to see. Questioning is never content free. It is about something, and it arises only when there is a gap in understanding, that is, a discrepancy between two or more ideas. Philosophical questioning, being about general and abstract matters, entails a discrepancy between two or more general and abstract ideas. If, therefore, we are to explain how viewing educational philosophy as questioning can be of value to practitioners, we have to determine which general and abstract ideas are to be involved in the questioning and indicate how those ideas might apply to the practical world of education.

To delimit the general and abstract ideas that are to be included, we will follow two guidelines. First, the ideas will be about educational practice although only in a general and abstract way. Thereby, they will be at least of general importance for particular practitioners. Second, the ideas will be justifiable to a wide range of educational philosophers. While this guideline does not imply that the ideas will be true, it does help ensure that the study of educational philosophy can lead to settled principles for educators rather than to ideas liable to contention among philosophers and confusion and uncertainty among educators.

An idea about educational practice that has to be universally accepted is that an educator is an interpersonal agent. That is, he or she is a person who does things that directly or indirectly influence some other doer of things. This is true because any practitioner performs a public function, thereby affecting members of the public. It is true also because educational practitioners always interact, indirectly if not directly, with students and often interact with each other. This holds whether educators are school teachers, counselors, or administrators. Another widely acceptable idea about educational practice was indicated by our earlier claim that practitioners of any kind are rational agents. As practitioners, people are knowledgeable. They are cognizant of who they are, what they are doing and why, what are the ends sought through their actions, who are the agents with whom they are interacting, and what are the immediate outcomes of their actions. After all, a major point of the professional training of practitioners is to prepare them to be informed about their actions.

An additional generally recognized idea about educational practitioners is that they, like practitioners of any other kind, act freely. No factor or factors beyond a given practitioner completely determine what he or she does. In other words, practitioners are not compelled, physically or psychologically, to do what they do; they are not prevented by external factors from doing what they want to do. More specifically, practitioners exercise control over their purposes and the actions by which they seek to attain their purposes. Practitioners have the goals that they have not because they have been made to have them but because they have rationally chosen them, that is, have chosen them for good reasons. They perform their actions not because they have been forced to perform them but because they have rationally decided upon them. In addition, practitioners do not pursue other goals, not because they are prevented from pursuing them, but because they do not have good reasons to. They do not perform other actions for the same reasons.

There is, however, a venerable position in philosophy that rejects the notion of free action. That position, called "determinism," maintains that no human action is within the control of its agent (Hospers, 1967, pp. 321–45). Any human action is caused ultimately by some external factor, most notably by God, nature, economic institutions, cultural practices, or psychological forces. Accordingly, because neither educators nor anybody else acts freely, the principle of free action is indefensible.

Even though the determinist's objection might initially appear to be tenable, it does not hold up under scrutiny, for it is self-defeating. If determinists are right in their objection, then they are not in control of their argument. Rather than advancing the objection because they have good reasons for it, they are forced to present it by some external factor. In addition, we are not in control of our responses to it. Far from accepting or rejecting it for good reasons, we are compelled to accept or reject it by some external factor. So, because the objection, even if true, can be neither accepted nor rejected for good reasons, it cannot, even if true, have the status of a rational argument. At most, it can have only the status of an external force acting upon our minds.

Another generally acceptable idea about the actions of practitioners is that such actions include major features besides interaction, knowledge, and freedom. Summarily stated, those charactistics are purpose, judgment, deliberation, and decision (Heslep, 1989, pp. 15–19; Heslep, 1995, pp. 26–32). Knowledgeable and free agents act for purposes that they choose on the basis of judgments about the worth of the proposed ends. In addition, such agents perform actions primarily as means for attaining their purposes, and they decide upon their actions through deliberation about which alternative courses of action are the right ones to perform.

While interaction, knowledge, freedom, purpose, and so forth are general features of any and all professional practice, each of these traits might differ in specifics from one kind of practice to another. Thus, the freedom specific to teaching might not be relevant to that specific to nursing. The knowledge involved in school administration differs from that involved in natural science. The judgmental standards pertinent to architecture are not proper to law.

Empirical evidence tends to show that practitioners value the freedom, knowledge, interpersonal relations, and other characteristics of their actions. The court cases and policies by which physicians, lawyers, teachers, architects, and other professionals have guarded their autonomy suggest their esteem for their knowledge and freedom. The pleasure and enrichment that professionals reputedly find in dealing with one another and in serving clients indicates that they value the interactive aspect of their work. Conceptual analysis also provides a basis for regarding practitioners as logically esteeming the traits of their actions. Because each and every practitioner sees the importance of these features in the performance of his or her particular professional function, any practitioner logically must esteem them for his or her self. Moreover, because each and every practitioner perceives the importance of these features for all other members of his or her specific practice—indeed for all other members of all other kinds of practice—any practitioner has to view them as worthy for his or her profession specifically and as worthy for all other professions in general.

But the characteristics of practice are more than objects of valuation by practitioners; they also are bases for certain professional rights, duties, and virtues of practitioners. Because practitioners need specific kinds of interaction, knowledge, freedom, judgment, and so forth to perform their public function, they may justifiably claim title to those features and thus for having their claims respected by the public as well as by one another. So, in education teachers have a right to academic freedom; administrators have a right to obtain resources for their schools and districts; and counselors have a right to confidentiality in working with their students.

Moreover, because each and every practitioner logically has to serve a specific public function through actions with certain traits, all are professionally obligated to perform that function and to maintain and foster conditions that support those traits. The duty of practitioners to perform their public functions means at least that they must serve the public when they do not have sufficient reason for not doing so. It does not mean that they must perform these duties when an actual public makes it unreasonably difficult, if not practically impossible, for them to do so, as in the case of inadequate salaries or of indiscriminate malpractice suits. Moreover, the duty of practitioners to maintain and foster the conditions that support the conceptually necessary features of their actions means that they are bound to encourage institutional arrangements that promote interpersonal relations in their fields; to engage in staff development and in-service training so as to expand and enhance their professional knowledge, skills, and appreciations; and to protect and encourage conditions favorable to their freedom, their choosing of purposes, and their deciding upon actions. No practitioner may decline to work for these conditions simply because he or she has no problems with the particular conditions of his or her actions. Other practitioners may need his or her help.

Finally, the chief characteristics of the actions of practitioners help constitute the foundation for their professional virtues. For instance, interaction calls for the virtues of politeness, sensitivity, caring, and friendliness toward clients and colleagues. Knowledgeability requires a love of truth, evidence, and understanding pertinent to professional affairs, as well as skills in obtaining knowledge relevant to such affairs. Freedom demands a disposition to act within the confines of professional standards and to accept responsibility for professional actions. Purpose entails the skill and disposition to formulate, with respect to judgmental standards and facts, worthy ends for professional actions. Deliberation involves the skill and disposition to make decisions based on the weighing of alternative courses of action with regard to their effectiveness and efficiency in obtaining projected ends and in view of their consistency with the professional values, rights, and duties of the practice of concern.

Because clients seek the services of practitioners and because the public at large makes provisions for such services, both clients and other members of the public logically respect the professional norms of practitioners. It would be silly to request the services of practitioners with known standards and then hold those standards in contempt, and it would be ridiculous for a public to establish professions and then denounce the norms entailed by the practices of those professions. Needless to say, not every actual client *seeks* professional services. Emotionally disturbed persons are sometimes made to see psychiatrists. Infants have no choice about seeing doctors. Students often have no choice about attending school, and parents occasionally are made to send their children to school. In these and related situations, however, persons other than the actual clients seek the services of practitioners on behalf of the clients. Thus, parents or public officials secure services for children or other dependents, and public officials sometimes override the decisions of parents and obtain services for the presumed good of the latter's children.

But if clients and the public at large logically must respect the values, rights, duties, and virtues of practitioners, practitioners have to recognize that the major traits of their actions are major traits also of the actions of clients and the public at large and, thus, that the latter traits give rise to norms that must be respected by practitioners. Like practitioners, clients and other members of the public are agents of interpersonal, informed, and free actions, and as such agents, they form purposes based on judgments and decide upon actions through deliberation. Accordingly, clients and the public at large logically have values, rights, duties, and virtues generically the same as norms had by practitioners. It follows that practitioners logically must respect these standards of clients and other members of the public. In truth, it follows that they have to look favorably upon the values, rights, duties, and virtues that any person has by being an agent of interpersonal, knowledgeable, and free action. In the respect that practitioners share values, rights, duties, and virtues with all other agents of interpersonal, informed, and free action, practitioners and the latter agents are equal to one another. This is, however, a general equality; it may not hold in specific circumstances. Thus, practitioners conceptually are superior to their clients with regards to providing professional services, and clients are likely to be superior to practitioners in matters beyond the latter's specialties.

In the field of education, the relationship between client and practitioner is special. Even though students engage in interpersonal action, they typically lack the powers of knowledge, judgment, and deliberation to act in an informed way. Hence, they sometimes act impulsively or under compulsion. While students might value freedom or make claims to it, they might not be likely to appreciate knowledge, judgment, and deliberation. In this respect, then, students are not even generally equal to teachers and administrators as agents of interpersonal, knowledgeable and free action. Nevertheless, in the respect that students may become mature agents of such action, they are prospective mature agents. Because educators logically see their students as future mature agents, they recognize that they logically should have in the future the norms of interpersonal, knowledgeable, and free action that they do not presently possess. Hence, the general equality between student and educator is potential, even if not actual.

That practitioners, clients, and the public at large are, prospectively as well as occurrently, agents of interpersonal, knowledgeable, and free actions has great moral significance (Heslep, 1995, pp. 26–44). First of all, their being agents of such actions means that they are moral agents. We all allow that moral agents are subject to praise and blame, and we hold that people are not liable to either unless they act knowingly and freely. Informed and free doers, however, need not be moral agents. If a knowing and free action influences only its agent, it is of prudential, not moral, significance. Such an action is of moral importance only when it is interpersonal. Thus, practitioners, clients, and other members of the public are moral agents in the respect that they are doers of interpersonal, informed, and free actions. The second point is that the norms that apply to practitioners, clients, and all other agents of moral actions are moral standards. That is, the values, rights, duties, and virtues related to the interactiveness, knowledge, freedom, purposefulness, and the other generic features of moral action are moral values, rights, duties, and virtues. They are the norms of moral agency.

The third point is that all practitioners, clients, and indeed all other moral agents logically must act consistently with the norms of moral agency. The reason why is that moral agents are conceptually committed to the standards governing their actions in preference to all other kinds of standards, whether prudential, religious, political, legal, economic, aesthetic, or educational. In their descriptive sense, moral norms are the standards to which people pledge themselves in interpersonal, knowledgeable, and free actions. By our analysis, moral agents are logically committed to what we have called the norms of moral agency. Because of ignorance or intellectual confusion, however, they in reality may pay allegiance to other standards, thereby assuming moral norms conceptually inappropriate to moral agents. Given the superiority of moral standards, regardless of their specific content, people logically can violate their religious, economic, political, or aesthetic principles on moral grounds, but they logically cannot violate their moral standards on religious, economic, political, or aesthetic grounds. So, because moral agents conceptually must follow the norms of moral agency, they logically must reject any principles opposed to those norms.

Clearly, we have found ideas that may serve as the content of the study of educational philosophy that purports to approach the subject as a matter of questioning; for our ideas about the chief traits of moral actions in general and professional practice specifically suggest questions about educational practice especially. For convenience, we will note only a sampler of suggested questions: Which conceptions of education are consistent with the features and norms of moral action including professional practice? Which curricula are consistent with the norms of such action? Which interactions, knowledge, freedom, purposes, judgments, actions, and deliberations are special to teachers, to students, and to administrators? Which values, rights, duties, and virtues are special to teachers, to students, and to administrators? Which traits and norms of moral action pertain specifically to parents, other community members, and the public at large?

In addressing these and other questions posed by the characteristics and norms of moral action, educators might discover that these characteristics and norms concord with certain democratic principles and policies (Heslep, 1989, pp. 69–78) and with major aspects of American culture and society (Heslep, 1995, pp. 45–63). Nevertheless, educators also are liable to arrive at answers opposed to their professional common sense. For instance, they might determine that what counts in their society as education is at odds with the features and norms of moral action; that the legal rights and duties of educators, students, parents, and others oppose the norms of moral action; and that the official ethical codes of their professional organizations are contrary to the norms of moral action.

Even if students of educational philosophy do learn that the traits and norms of moral action sometimes are opposed to professional common sense, they should not conclude thereby that the latter does not merit their serious attention. Professional common sense rests upon a wealth of practical knowledge and experience. It usually enables practitioners to deal with routine matters in effective ways. In addition, it provides action guides for practitioners faced with urgent problems and thus without time for philosophical reflection. That educators can use professional common sense in handling routine matters and might have to employ it in making urgent decisions means that educators neither always need nor always can have a profound understanding of their practical affairs. There are occasions, however, when educators can have and must have an underlying grasp of such affairs; those are situations where time is available for extended questioning and where problems are unfamiliar. Because practical wisdom is highly reflective, it usually takes more time than the reasoning of professional common sense. But because of its concern with the general features and norms of moral action, it does enable educators to apply those features and norms to educational situations that are more or less unfamiliar.

While approaching educational philosophy through the study of the characteristics and standards of moral agency enables students to learn much about ethics, it seems to put them in a position of learning very little about logic, metaphysics, and epistemology. At least, our discussion of this route gives greater attention to moral matters than it does to those of logic, metaphysics, and epistemology. It is doubtful, however, that our proposed way for studying educational philosophy unduly emphasizes the moral dimensions of educational practice. Because it is the conceptual nature of such practice to be a species of moral action, it would be unjustifiable to play down or ignore the moral aspects of the practice. If we discussed the moral facets of education without locating them in an educational context, we would focus upon the moral unjustifiably. Moreover, if we looked at the moral dimensions of educational practice while disregarding logical, metaphysical, or epistemological issues involved in them, we would be overly stressing the moral. Our approach, however, does not appear to be guilty on either count. The understanding that any educator needs will always involve normative questions, and while it will not exclude logical, metaphysical, and epistemological issues, it will include them only as a consideration of normative questions leads to them. Thus, to study logical, metaphysical, and epistemological questions in educational philosophy in a balanced way is to place them within the moral framework of educational practice, which is what our proposed approach attempts to do.

We may illustrate the practical import of our intent here by reference to epistemology. That our statements regarding knowledge have been superficial does not mean that they are totally benign. They plainly allow that there are different types of knowledge, for instance, practical, scientific, mathematical, and theological. At the same time, they allow that these different sorts are had by various methods and may or may not compete with each other. While the statements do not set forth definitions of knowledge and truth, they implicitly accept ordinary definitions of them, for example: Knowledge is truth claims for which we have adequate reasons; truth in one sense is the way things are; in another sense it is a quality of a statement. Our references to knowledge also allow that there are other definitions that may or may not agree with ordinary ones. But while the references appear to be relatively open on epistemology, they do not intend that one theory of knowledge is necessarily just as good or bad as any other. What they do recognize, however, is that educators may leave the inquiry into fundamental epistemological questions to philosophers, scientists, jurists, poets, and others with profound concerns about knowledge. Hence, when they have to face those issues in their search for understanding about their goals and actions, they can look to such thinkers for help. Educators, of course, may seek help from philosophers also when they encounter logical, metaphysical, and moral difficulties that they cannot resolve on their own.

QUESTIONS ABOUT CASES

But even if prospective and occurrent educators approach educational philosophy by learning to pose questions about educational purposes and actions within the framework of moral agency, they need not find the subject of sufficient value for themselves when they eventually engage in educational practice. They might learn to raise questions about education in general rather than about the particular educational situations in which they will find themselves as practitioners. If, therefore, the study of educational philosophy is to satisfy the need of educators to understand their purposes and actions in particular contexts, it must prepare them specifically to address questions about such contexts. This finding is not novel. It reflects an interest in the use of case analysis in educational studies that has emerged in recent years (Strike and Soltis, 1985; Shulman, 1992; Sykes and Bird, 1992; Johnston and Wetherill, 1995).

One way for the study of educational philosophy to help students in this regard is for it to undertake a close questioning of a variety of textbook cases. While the cases to be examined inevitably will share certain characteristics, they should be sufficiently different from one other that each has to be understood within the framework of moral agency without reference to any of the others. They may be like this if each is different both in kind and in particulars from the others. It is not necessary for the cases to be real; it is enough if they are realistic. They may be composites drawn from materials in educational research, media reports, and personal experience.

PROCEDURAL

The argument presented in these two chapters has held that the study of educational philosophy may have practical value for student educators. More specifically, it has maintained that the examination of practical cases within the philosophical framework of moral agency helps student educators learn to query and thus to understand the situations in which they will work.

Each of the next five chapters will feature a particular case. While the cases have been constructed to be quite different from one another, a common procedure may be followed in an investigation of them all. That procedure includes a description of the background of the case, a description of the case itself, an identification of the central topic or topics of the case, a specification of the traits of moral agency as they appear in the case, an application of the norms of moral agency to the case, and a statement of what morally needs to be done in the case. Of these steps, the one identifying a case's central topic or topics requires explanation. By the central topic or topics of a case, I mean the theme or themes that run throughout the case, thereby providing the latter with a focus. This focus in turn provides a reference point for specifying the characteristics of moral agency as they appear in the case. In some of the cases, the identification of central topics is relatively easy; in others, it is relatively difficult. Either way, I provide reasons for regarding topics as central. Typically, I take a topic to be central if I find that all or nearly all elements in the relevant case are covered by that topic. For pedagogical convenience, each of the cases to be examined has only one central theme.

In discussing the cases in this book, I pose questions related to all major characteristics and standards of moral agency, and I sometimes become involved in complex arguments. Moreover, I draw conclusions that might appear to be beyond dispute. I do not mean, however, for students to think that philosophical thought in educational practice always has to be extensive and involved. Sometimes such thought might bear on only one or two features and norms and can be considered relatively simple. In addition, I do not intend for students to regard my conclusions as beyond challenge. When students suspect that conclusions are poorly supported by the analyses from which they are drawn, students should review those analyses and conclusions and, if they find mistakes in the analyses or conclusions, should correct the errors. Student criticism of my case discussions is indicative of the questioning that the discussions seek to promote.

While the raising of questions about realistic textbook cases can help prepare students to gain a basic understanding of the particular and concrete situations that they will face as practitioners, it should not be the last step in their learning to acquire such understanding. Even if realistic textbook cases enable students to ponder the relevance of the traits and norms of moral agency to a range of particular situations, they cannot help students to query full-fledged practical situations. Such situations, as explained earlier, are concrete as well as particular. Textbook cases, however, are necessarily abstract. When one deals with a situation that is particular and abstract, one may examine it without the inevitable possibility of its changing, and one may make analyses, choices, and decisions without doing harm in the real world. But when one deals with a situation that is concrete as well as particular, one cannot make it stand still while one reflects upon it, and one might make wrong analyses, choices, and decisions that bring harm to real people and conditions. Ultimately, then, students who will have learned to probe textbook cases within the framework of moral agency will need to have some supervised experience in addressing concrete situations within that framework. They can have this experience during practice teaching, mentoring, or clinical training. While the supervision of the experience would appropriately come from a person who teaches educational philosophy, it does not have to. It may come from any supervisor of would-be or actual educators who is capable of practical moral wisdom, that is, who is disposed to question real educational situations from the standpoint of moral agency. So, the main point about examining textbook cases is not that the questioning will not completely prepare students to become practitioners capable of practical wisdom. The point, rather, is that it will ready students to benefit from experience that can make them capable of such wisdom.

3

A Mission Statement Committee Meeting

In the United States, educators frequently engage in discussions with parents, school board members, and other members of the public. While those discussions typically cover bread and butter matters, for instance, teenage pregnancy, drugs, student achievement, and budgets, they occasionally raise the question of what kind of education schools should offer. It is fitting that they address this issue even if only from time to time. Because the public authorizes and supports schools, it ought to have an idea of the education it wants them to provide. Moreover, school teachers and administrators can know what programs, methods, and materials to employ only if they know what their schools are supposed to be doing. Many school districts appear to recognize the importance of the question of the education their schools are to furnish because they draw up mission statements. In the language of those statements, the educational purpose of a school or school system is the major part, if not the whole, of its mission. While a mission statement might be largely the product of educators, with no wider or more thoughtful public input than perfunctory comments by the members of the involved district's board, it might be a product of a serious exchange between district educators and representatives of the district's public.

The following case centers around a portion of the dialogue among the members of a committee appointed to draw up a mission statement for the school system of Biekman County, which is fictional. Our goal is to examine the dialogue according to the traits and norms of moral agency. More specifically, we will seek to determine in what respects the dialogue's various suggestions about the system's educational goal logically include those features and standards. In addition, we will try to detect any modifications that might have to be made in the suggestions to keep them consistent with the standards.

INTRODUCTION TO BIEKMAN COUNTY

Biekman County includes the small cities of Eldred and Flores, several towns, and a large unincorporated rural area. Even though the county has straddled an interstate highway for forty years and lies only forty miles from the edge of a metropolis, it has undergone very little change in recent times. The major economic source still is agriculture. The citizens engaged in the professions continue to be small in number and located mainly in Eldred and Flores. Lately, a few new professionals have taken up residence in the town of Springhill, which borders Hooten County, the exurban sprawl lying between Biekman and the nearby metropolis, but those professionals have their practices in Hooten. Except for low-wage employment at the convenience stores, automobile service centers, and motels near Biekman's two clover-leaf intersections, the interstate has generated no business for the area. The vast majority of the rural population has stayed white and poor while the African American population largely has remained small, urban, and lower middle class. A half dozen oriental families lately have joined the county's business class. The professional people's children continue to go to college and never return, while most of the other children do not go to college and usually remain in the county. Those who stay work on farms, in forests, or for retail businesses, or they become supported by public assistance. Religious affiliation remains widespread and predominantly Protestant.

Two notable changes recently occurred in Biekman County related to its schools. Since 1920, Eldred and Flores each had an independent school system, which recently consisted of one high school, two middle schools, and two elementary schools. The county's school system had been of a similar size and structure. During the past year, however, the citizens of each of the two cities and the other citizens of the county voted to merge the three systems. They believed that the union would keep down expenses and taxes. The other change was the appointment of the superintendent for the Biekman County United School System. To prevent even the appearance of favoritism, the members of the newly established board of education agreed among themselves that none of the previous three incumbent superintendents should become head of the new system. After a formal search for and review of candidates, the board members appointed Henry Moore, an associate superintendent of another county's school system. Moore had grown up on a farm in Biekman County and attended county schools. After college, he had taught social studies in Eldred's high school for several years and then obtained professional training as a school administrator. After serving as assistant principal and then as principal of one of the Eldred middle schools, he had taken the job as associate superintendent.

While Superintendent Moore was quite aware of Biekman County's situation, he presumed that the county might change significantly in the foreseeable future. The county where he had been associate superintendent had been unexpectedly transformed from rural to a mix of exurban and rural. Thus, he wanted to prepare the new school system for whatever major changes were likely to occur. Superintendent Moore also was aware that Biekman's citizens were watching to see if he would steer the new system to benefit Eldred and Flores at the expense of the rest of the county or the reverse. Accordingly, he further wanted to ensure that the system would benefit primarily the whole county, not just some part of it. To address these areas of concern, the superintendent appointed a committee with broad representation to formulate a mission statement for the system. The members of the committee were as follows: Ernest Gibbs, the president of the county business association; the Reverend Buford Johnson, the president of the county clerical alliance; Carl Schott, the head of the county milk producers association; Wilbur Jasper, owner of the county's largest row-crop farm; Elizabeth Spivak, the president of the school parents organization; Marlene Reid, the principal of Springhill Elementary School; Jessica Fowler, the chair of the social science department at Flores High School; and Mary Hytinck, assistant superintendent.

DISCUSSION BY THE MISSION STATEMENT COMMITTEE

Ms. Hytinck: As Superintendent Moore mentioned a while ago at our organizational meeting, he asked me to preside at this committee's meetings. He also informed me during the break, in no uncertain words, that I am to preside at these meetings but I am not to lead them. He wants the mission statement to be yours. Of course, he is responsible to the Board of Education and the public for this committee, so he will want to sign off on whatever statement you put together and present it to the board for its review. He wants the statement to include at its center the kind of education that the schools are to furnish our children, but he has no preconceived specific ideas about what that education should be. As he explained at our preliminary meeting, he has two guidelines for you to follow but nothing else. Those guidelines, you might remember, are that we consider likely changes in Biekman County and that we keep in mind that the new school system is to serve all the children of all the county. At any rate, this meeting, as I understand our procedure, is to be exploratory. We are to find out what kind of ideas you might have for the schools' mission. At another meeting in a couple of weeks you can make any changes in those ideas you think necessary and use them for drawing up a formal statement. Okay, I think we're ready to open the discussion.

Mr. Jasper: I remember Superintendent Moore saying that he would like for us to follow those guidelines, but I wonder if he should have included another guideline?

Ms. Hytinck: That would be what, Wilbur?

Mr. Jasper: Well, the major reason for merging the school systems was to be able to hold down expenses and taxes. So shouldn't we be guided by the idea that whatever education we set for the new school system should not require any increase in expenses and taxes?

Ms. Hytinck: Wilbur, Superintendent Moore is certainly aware of the school expense issue. He has already reduced administrative overhead from what it was two years ago, and he is looking for other ways to make the administration of the united school system even less expensive. However, he did not think it necessary to include an expense guideline for your mission statement. He believes that the members of this committee are prudent enough to keep the statement within the bounds of what the people of Biekman County are willing to support.

Mr. Gibbs: Well, I think you can rest assured that we won't allow school expenses to be more than we can bear. At the same time, however, I don't want to appear to be opposed to good education. After all, I have children attending school here. But I do think that the schools should be able to provide a decent education for all at an affordable cost.

Ms. Spivak: Ernie, those are good points, and all of us probably agree with them. Why don't we then forget about costs for the time being and think about what the schools ought to be doing? I've talked with lots of parents this past year, and the one thing about them that has most impressed me is that they hope the schools will give their children a good education, one that will prepare them to do well in life.

Mr. Schott: Well, I don't know about the rest of you, but I have doubts that schools are going to be able to help all the kids in this county get ahead in life. Take the dairy farming business here. As you know, dairy farming is a hard life, but we have been able to make a living from it. We never needed the schools to do anything for us other than teach our kids reading, writing, arithmetic, and citizenship. But in the last fifteen years, things have been changing for the worse. People aren't drinking as much milk and eating as much butter and cheese as they used to. Equipment and fertilizer costs keep climbing. And now the government is threatening to cut back on price supports. I don't believe the milk farmers we have in this county will be able to survive another generation. Their operations are too small, and they'll lose out to the giant operators in other places. So I just don't know how the schools are going to do a lot for the dairy farmers' kids.

Mr. Jasper: You're right, Carl, and much of what you're saying holds for many of the dirt farmers here. Besides all the troubles that you have mentioned, we're also facing a lot of foreign competition. It seems like every country in the world wants to grow wheat and soy beans. I seriously doubt that anyone with less than a thousand acres will be able to make a go of row cropping after the next ten years or so. Also, some of my acquaintances have hinted that their kids decided to go on welfare rather than try to eke out a living on a few hundred acres. I can't blame them in a way. These are decent kids; they're not lazy or afraid of work. They just don't see a future in the life they're used to. So, maybe what Carl and I are saying is that the only thing the schools here can do for a lot of the county's children is get them to know their basic subjects and their rights and responsibilities as citizens.

Ms. Reid: Wilbur, I deeply respect the serious concern that you and Carl have for the future of rural children here, but I wonder if you aren't selling them short. Let me explain. These kids aren't helpless; they don't have to sit passively by while waiting for a better life to appear. Farming and welfare are not their only choices. There are hundreds of jobs available less than an hour's drive away. Maybe the problem for these kids, then, is that we have not broadened their awareness of job opportunities. Maybe this is something the schools can do for them.

Mr. Schott: I've heard other places too that there are jobs not far away, and I suppose that the schools could tell students about them, maybe even train them for the jobs. But I don't think you understand some important things about those jobs. Most of them are minimum wage; they don't pay enough for a fellow to support his family. Also, the better paying ones probably want a pretty good education, training at a technical school or college. But even if a struggling farmer could afford to send his children to some kind of higher institution, they might not be cut out for it or wouldn't want to go to it.

Rev. Johnson: I've been listening to you people and really learning a lot. I'm proud and fortunate to be working with you. But if you would permit me, I want to suggest that there might be some matters besides jobs for the schools to worry about. As you know, a minister has to counsel people about problems that are not always made public. I can't give you any specifics, of course, but I can tell you that there have been more and more problems in families here. More than half the young ones who get married now wind up divorced in just a few years. This helps make a growing number of single mothers who have to have their mothers look after their babies or who have to stay at home and go on welfare. In addition, we are having more and more unmarried teenage girls who are having babies. I also have talked with a number of wives who have been beaten by their husbands, and I've heard of a lot of grief caused by boys using drugs and doing violence to their parents. I'm not saying that these problems include most families in the county, but I am saying that they are more numerous than I remember when I first came here fifteen years ago. I really think our schools ought to do something about the moral character of their students. Those kids certainly are not learning any morals from all the sex and violence they watch on television.

Ms. Reid: Reverend, you know a lot more about the family troubles in this county than I do, but what you say agrees with what I have heard from the schools. The impression that I get from dealing with parents at Springhill is consistent with the picture that you have drawn. And my acquaintances at the high schools have expressed concerns similar to yours. They tell me that discipline problems in their schools have gotten to where they are starting to interfere with classroom instruction. Only last week, there were several instances in the high schools where students cursed at their teachers. In any event, if we want to have concrete facts about adolescent problems in the county, we can ask the social work agency for them.

Ms. Fowler: Look, I'm just a department head who has lived here for only five years; I don't have nearly as much knowledge about Biekman County as the rest of you. But I don't find my students all that bad, and not all of them are nerds or governor's award winners. It's my guess that if teachers offer materials and content in which their students are interested, they won't have a lot of trouble from them. I wouldn't blame students for becoming bored and disruptive if I presented them with aspects of history or economics in which they weren't interested. Probably any subject has features that can be interesting to any student, even mathematics. Of course, we can't know how to teach to student interests if we don't know what they are, and we can't know what they are unless we ask students what they are interested in. But there is a related problem for this committee. We're sitting here trying to figure out what the schools of this county should be doing for all its students, but we are attempting to do this without talking to students. There are no students on this committee. How can we know how the schools can serve them if we don't hear from them? Would it be possible to hear from some students at a future meeting?

Ms. Hytinck: Superintendent Moore will leave it to this committee to decide whether or not to have students appear before it. He did consider appointing one or two students to the committee but chose not to. As you know, students are not mature. Even those who are very thoughtful lack the experience needed for making sound judgments. So the superintendent thought it might be impossible to appoint one or two students who could speak for all or most of them. Nevertheless, he does believe that student input might give us some insights we otherwise would miss.

Mr. Gibbs: I don't have any objection to hearing from some students, although I'm a bit skeptical that something should be taught only if it is something they are interested in. As Reverend Johnson said, they watch a lot of trash on television, but I seriously doubt we want them to study that in school. They change their minds all the time. What if they are interested in something today and don't care about it tomorrow? Are we suppose to change subjects whenever students change interests? That sounds like a recipe for chaos. At any rate, if we we are to hear from students, let's have at least one representing those going off to college and some representing those with other ambitions. In addition, I want to comment on some things said earlier. Character education is something all our students can stand, but that is a long-term matter. We might need to do something urgent for students we've now got. From what Reverend Johnson said, I gather that there are pregnant unmarried students. What happens to them when they have their babies? Do we add those students to the welfare roll and forget them until their babies grow up and have more illegitimate babies? Or do we try to get them to support themselves and have no more chldren until they are married?

Ms. Reid: Ernie, those are great questions, and I happen to know of schools in other districts that have tried to answer them. They have put in place programs for teaching student mothers about caring for their children, about the importance of not having more children until marriage, and about the importance of learning job skills. But I must warn you, Ernie, that those programs will cost money. Additional staff will be needed to work with student mothers, and the occupational studies program here would have to be upgraded. Moreover, the girls are only a part of the problem. The fathers, at least those who are students, have to learn about their responsibilities as fathers, and they should gain job skills, too. We also would have to work with the parents of these student parents to get their support and cooperation. This would require a liaison social worker. Biekman may be a poor county, but it seems to have expensive problems.

Ms. Fowler: Maybe I'm naive, but I don't think that this expense thing is impossible. There are some state funds available for family education, and there are some federal funds for occupational studies. The superintendent's office can check on those. What we need to be equally concerned with, however, is the long run. There are signs in Springhill that this county will gain more professional people as Hooten County becomes more crowded and expensive. That means our schools will have to grow, which means we will need more revenue. Perhaps we should think about attracting some industry here to help shore up our tax base. We have a few things going for us to do that. We're near a giant city and we're right on an interstate. But from what I've read, we'll have to strengthen our schools if we are to get any plants to locate here. Companies want their workers to be able to have a good education. They also would want this county to supply them with good workers.

Mr. Jasper: It sounds to me like we're in a bind. We have to spend more money to save some. I don't know if we would get a worthwhile return on the increase in spending. Still, I like the idea of bringing in industry as a way of easing the tax load. What about you, Carl?

Mr. Schott: It's okay with me, I suppose. If our kids can't enjoy a future in farming, I guess they'll have to settle for learning to work in industry.

Ms. Hytinck: Maybe this is a good time to take stock of what we've been saying. We've had a long evening. There are a lot of ideas on the table, and they cover a broad range of topics. Also, I don't sense any deep divisions in your thinking. But before I go any further, I want to make sure that I am not cutting anyone off from discussion at this point. Are there more suggestions that someone wants to make before I try pulling your thoughts together? Are there any comments on the ideas already expressed?

Rev. Johnson: Yes, please. I want to return for a moment to the need for moral character education, which was lost in our concern with finding expedients for dealing with pressing social problems. But now that Ms. Fowler has pointed out that we need to think about the long term in the economic growth of this county, I believe we should resume thinking also about the long term in the moral development of our children. We will continue to have social problems in this county until our children start to acquire the right sort of moral habits. So the longer we put off their moral education, the longer we will have social problems. Character building may not have short-term benefits, but we cannot afford to put it off. Thank you.

Ms. Hytinck: Reverend, nobody could say that any better than you. I am positive we will not lose sight again of the need for character education. Now, are there any other opinions to be heard at this time? Your silence tells me that we may proceed with the summary.

Plainly, all of you agree that Biekman County has to strengthen its economic base if its students, as well as its other citizens, are to have a decent life here. At least, you seemed to acknowledge that many students right now don't have much to look forward to in the way of jobs and that the schools can't do all for their students that they need to if they don't have a larger tax source to draw from. Let me mention, however, that improving the economic structure of the county might not be appropriate as a part of the mission of the schools. I can assure you that Superintendent Moore would agree that the schools can help attract industry to the county and that he would be more than willing to work with the county's leaders to obtain economic growth. But I believe that he will see economic growth as a part of the county's mission rather than as a part of the schools'. What you can do eventually is attach a statement of your ideas about the need for a larger tax base with your mission statement. At any rate, you might want to return to this after I have finished with this summary.

According to my notes, these are your other suggestions. I won't attempt to put them in your exact words, but I will try to make sure that I put them in words that say what you intend.

1. Your ideas about the need for moral education might be put this way: The schools are to instill their students with a character for a worthwhile life.

2. Your suggestions about the discipline situation might go this way: The schools are to teach students their responsibilities to each other, school officials, their families, and the public.

3. What you said about job ambitions might be summed up in this fashion: The schools are to prepare students to pursue careers of their choice.

4. Your comments on student pregnancy and parenthood might be broadened a bit and put this way: The schools are to help students with their needs to become responsible parents and to become self-supporting.

I won't swear that I have covered everything that you have discussed so far, and I certainly won't claim that my phrasing of what you said is accurate or complete. Moreover, I suppose there might be a few other notions that you all want to consider for our mission statement. But I do think it is time to bring this meeting to a close. Before the next meeting, please go over my summary. You can change it however you like at the beginning of the next meeting and then raise whatever other ideas you might have. Before leaving that meeting, however, you will have to produce at least a rough draft of your mission statement. So come prepared to stay late!

IDENTIFICATION OF THE CENTRAL TOPIC

We now want to examine the discussion by the Mission Statement Committee within the framework of moral agency. In investigating the discussion, we will find it helpful to determine if there is some topic, or theme, that encompasses all others. Such a topic would serve as an organizing point for our analysis. Plainly, the topic that dominates the discussion is the mission of the Biekman County schools, which, in effect, is the education that those schools are to provide. Let us, then, begin our analysis by examining what the committee says about that education.

Even though the Mission Statement Commmittee does not fully and clearly explain what education it intends for the students of Biekman County to have, it does express notions that are suggestive of what that education might be. Ms. Spivak, the head of the school parents association, refers to a "good" education, or one that prepares students to do well in life. Unfortunately, she does not explain what it means to do well in life any more than she indicates what she means by a bad education or an education in the nonjudgmental sense of the term. It might be for her that doing well in life is, among other possibilities, performing one's social roles properly, becoming materially prosperous within the bounds of the law, or simply being happy. By contrast Mr. Schott and Mr. Jasper, the farmers, propose a minimal education, or one that provides instruction in the academic fundamentals and in citizenship. Not seeing any hope for a prosperous life for the children of most of the county's farmers, they do not especially mean for this education to help students to do well in life; they presumably intend for it mainly to prepare students to get by in life.

Reverend Johnson does not aim to propose a total education for the children of Biekman County; he means only to recommend moral education as an essential part of whatever education the committee settles upon. Even though he does cite several types of conduct that he takes to be wrong, he does not mention what moral principles he holds. One suspects, however, that whatever moral orientation he assumes is largely shared by most, if not all, other members of the committee. Ms. Reid, the principal, overtly agrees with his remarks and asks only that classroom discipline also be a part of whatever education the committee agrees upon. Moreover, no one expresses a concern that Reverend Johnson's moral principles might not be suitable for the students of the county's schools.

While Mr. Gibbs, who represents the mercantile and financial views of the county, states no objections to any of the ideas about education mentioned above, he tends to frame his notion of education for the county's schools in terms not employed by the other committee members. In brief, he speaks of education as preparing students to pursue careers. He emphatically wants the schools to enable students to pursue their career ambitions, and he appears to assume that the schools will provide different programs to help the students attain this end. That is, there will be a program for students needing to go to college, one for those wanting to attend a vocational technical school, and one for those seeking employment upon finishing high school. While Mr. Gibbs seems to see education for moral character, classroom discipline, and citizenship as important for Biekman County's schools, he probably does not regard it as the focal point of the schools. He likely regards it as a necessary supplement to career education.

Other remarks by committee members intimate other possible views of education for the county. While the plea by Ms. Fowler for student input was not a statement of what education specifically should be in the schools, it did suggest that whatever else that education should be, it should be something of interest to students. Mr. Gibbs, at least, took the plea to have this meaning, for he wondered how the schools could have a curriculum that was both stable and oriented to student interests. In her summary statement No. 4, Ms. Hytinck interprets the committee's discussion as holding that Biekman's schools should prepare students to become economically self-supporting. While this statement relates especially to students at risk of becoming social dependencies, it seems to be consistent with the kinds of education advocated by Ms. Spivak and Mr. Gibbs. That is, one assumes that for Ms. Spivak doing well in life likely includes economic independence and that for Mr. Gibbs a career definitely includes such independence as a norm.

Yet, if the committee desires the students of Biekman County to learn to be economically self-supporting, does it also want them to learn to be autonomous in other respects? Ms. Reid, it will be remembered, insisted that the schools should enable students to make career choices and decisions; Mr. Gibbs held that the schools should prepare students to pursue their career ambitions, which entail choices and decisions. But if the committee wants students to learn to be not only economically independent but also autonomous in choosing careers and deciding how to pursue them, might it not further think that they should become autonomous in general? If autonomy is good in the economic sector of life, why not also in religious, political, social, aesthetic, sexual, and all other sectors? Superintendent Moore's guideline about impending changes in the county certainly allows for an education that encourages students to be generally autonomous. Because nobody knows what specific changes will occur, the committee will do well in wanting students to be able to make choices and decisions with respect to those changes, whatever they are. Moreover, because the changes in Biekman County in the next five to ten years will not be the last changes there or elsewhere in the future lives of its students, the committee perhaps should want students to learn to make choices and decisions throughout their lives.

THE RELEVANCE OF MORAL AGENCY

In setting forth their various ideas on education for the Biekman County Unified School System, the members of the Mission Statement Committee have not relied upon educational theory or research findings. Instead, they have received guidance principally from their store of information about the practices, the behavior, and the values of the county's people, from their impressions about the nearby metropolitan area, from their grasp of agricultural trends, from their first-hand experience with the local schools, and from their personal points of view and preferences. While these perceptions, facts, and attitudes constitute a portion of what might pass for the common sense of Biekman County, they have not led the committee members to have, at least initially, uniform agreement over what education the local schools should provide. Thus, the view of Mr. Schott and Mr. Jasper differs from Ms. Spivak's. Despite their differences, however, the committee members hope to develop a consensus on the school system's mission. Ms. Hytinck surely will be working to secure a view of education that will be acceptable to all, including Superintendent Moore.

But before the committee members attempt to reach agreement on a mission statement, they should reflect upon the various views they have already expressed. Is any of their ideas on education worthwhile? If so, by what measure? While consensus in committee work is often desirable, it alone does not ensure that a committee's work is otherwise estimable. Thus, one can easily imagine a committee in Nazi Germany that was in total accord on an educational policy that fostered in students vicious character traits, for instance, feelings of racial superiority and hatred. If not consensus, however, what standard or standards should the Biekman County committee members use in recasting their thoughts on their schools' mission? We cannot say that the members will scrutinize their educational ideas when they reassemble after the break or at another meeting. We can say, however, that if they do, they will be in a position to guide themselves by the norms of moral agency. We can say this because their educational views entail the features of moral agency and thus the norms associated with those features.

THE TRAITS OF MORAL AGENCY

Moral agency, we have noted, has several central characteristics: interpersonal, cognizant, free, purposive, judgmental, decisive, and deliberative. All of them are involved in the educational views put forth by the members of the Mission Statement Committee.

Interpersonal

In their educational views the members certainly allow that the students of Biekman County are parties to interpersonal actions, for they plainly refer to the students as influencing or being affected by one another, their teachers, and their parents. But while the members focus on current, direct, and face-to-face interpersonal actions involving students, they also allow that some interpersonal actions involving students—indeed, some of the most important ones—are futuristic, indirect, and remote. What the students do now in school probably will have consequences in their future lives as well as in the lives of other agents with whom the students will interact in the future. For instance, students who do not presently learn to be financially self-supporting might face material hardship and impose social and tax burdens upon those people who will be economically self-sufficient. The foreseeable disappearance of the agricultural way of life shared by many of the students is, according to Mr. Schott and Mr. Jasper, more an outcome filtering down from policies made in legislatures and markets than a result of actions immediately involving the farmers of Biekman County. In addition, the impending changes in the county that will alter the future lives of students are likely to occur mainly because of choices and decisions made in distant corporate headquarters and by real estate investors and developers located far beyond the county's boundaries. In sum, the Mission Statement Committee members take the bulk of the lives of the students to include interpersonal action.

Knowledge

There is no doubt that knowledge occupies a place in the different educational views of the committee members. Mr. Schott's and Mr.

Jasper's proposal for students to learn to "get by" in life explicitly mentions the learning of basic academic subjects and of citizenship, but the proposal implicitly allows too that students must acquire the common sense that is necessary for getting by. While Ms. Spivak's idea that Biekman County's students should learn to do well in life logically allows that they must acquire academic fundamentals, knowledge of democratic citizenship, and common sense, it also has to grant that they ought to learn other cognitive matters too. At least a general knowledge of science and technology is important for doing well in the United States these days, and skills in critical thinking and problem solving also are important. Mr. Gibbs's recommendation that the county's schools help students to pursue their career ambitions presumably would include science, technology, and higher order cognitive skills, but it supposedly would contain, in addition, specialized knowledge that students might obtain in occupational studies, for instance, in advanced mathematics, natural science, computer science, and technical fields.

Freedom

That freedom is integral to the committee members' educational views is obvious in Ms. Reid's reminder to Mr. Jasper that the county's students are not helpless, that they can make life choices. Moreover, this feature of moral agency is present in Mr. Gibbs's reference to career ambitions. Even though some people seem driven in the pursuit of their ambitions, they are the exception. In most contexts, an ambition is something that one freely has and pursues. Finally, Ms. Fowler alludes to student freedom when she talks about the need for class subjects to be interesting. Studying a subject in which one has not even the least interest might be a condition of having to study it, whereas being interested in a subject might be a condition for freely learning it. To be sure, a person who studies a subject because of an overpowering interest in it does not freely study it, but one who studies it because of a noncompulsive interest in it does freely study it. It is this tie between student interests and their freedom that helps explain the focus of John Dewey and other educators upon student interests, for these educational thinkers regarded student freedom as possible only when subject matter was of interest to students.

Purposefulness and Judgment

Two other characteristics of moral agency that appear in the positions expressed by the committee members are purposefulness and judgment. The most obvious way in which purposefulness is embedded in these positions is that each of the positions is supposed to contribute to a statement of purpose, namely, the mission of Biekman County's schools. That these positions reflect any purpose held by students is problematic. Ms. Fowler's complaint that the committee has not sought input from students certainly intimates that the educational proposals do not necessarily reflect any goal of interest to students. On the other hand, the committee members do not seem opposed to obtaining at some future time student opinion on the schools' mission. One suspects, however, that most of the committee members initially considered the schools' mission as an end that students should want to attain but not necessarily one that students would want to attain. In other words, before Ms. Fowler raised the question of student interest, most of the members saw the schools' mission to be imposed upon the student body. But even if the committee members tended to see the schools' mission as something to be established without student advice, all of them appeared to try to conceive a mission that would serve the individual life goals of students, such as getting by or doing well in life or having a career of one's choice.

Purposes, of course, may be good or bad, better or worse. The way in which rational agents determine that their ends will be worthy or not is to subject them to normative judgment, which is, in its fully developed form, a process that establishes the value of something by a consideration of facts in the light of normative standards. Hence, any purpose that the Mission Statement Committee assigns to the Biekman County schools will be liable to judgment; any aim that any student has is also subject to judgment. In the discussion by the committee members, there is a shared concern that students are not mature in their ability to judge. They lack facts and experience; they frequently change their minds. Hence, they need adult guidance in choosing their respective life goals, and they need to depend upon the judgment of the committee members to construct the mission of the county's schools. But at the same time that the committee members regard students as immature, in varying degrees, in judgment, they allow that judgment is important for establishing purposes, including those of the county's schools and its individual students.

Decision and Deliberation

Decision and deliberation are the remaining major traits of moral agency that are embedded in the educational thinking of the Mission Statement Committee. While moral agents choose their goals on the basis of judgments, they decide upon the actions to attain their goals through deliberation. To decide is to select a course of action and follow it. To deliberate, however, is to weigh alternative courses of action so as to establish which is the right one to perform. Because real moral agents are imperfect, they might not actually relate their deliberations to their decisions in a logical way. They might become fascinated with deliberation for its own sake and never reach decisions. Or they might not decide upon courses of action other than those they have established through deliberation as the right ones to take. As moral agents, however, people should pursue whatever actions their deliberations lead to.

In their discussion of school costs and taxes, the members of the Mission Statement Committee commit themselves to deliberation, for they acknowledge that eventually alternative routes of action must be weighed so as to establish the right way for supporting whatever purpose they give to the county's schools. In some of their educational proposals, they also regard deliberation as relevant to the county's students. Mr. Jasper, for instance, refers to the children of some farmers as holding that depending upon public assistance is preferable to farming as a means of financial support. Moreover, because Mr. Gibbs plainly sees the programs of study to be offered by the schools as means for helping students to attain their career objectives, he presumably would grant that students, academic advisors, or parents need to weigh which programs are the right ones for which career objectives. Finally, if the committee members do want the county's students to become at least economically self-supporting and perhaps autonomous in all other ways, they have to allow that the students must learn to be not only decisive but also deliberative. To be independent, people must make their own decisions, but they will not be independent long if they do not ground their decisions on deliberation.

THE NORMS OF MORAL AGENCY

Because the Mission Statement Committee members must recognize, upon reflection, that they have at least implicitly framed their educational proposals in terms of the characteristics of moral agency, they must recognize also, upon further reflection, that they have committed themselves to the norms of moral agency. Those criteria, it will be remembered, are the appreciation of, the right to, and the duty to support and foster the features of moral agency. In other words, the committee members theoretically must concede that the students of Biekman County should develop into mature moral agents, that is, should learn to value the traits of moral agency, become aware of and exercise their rights to those traits, and become mindful of their duty to maintain and encourage conditions of moral agency. In conceding this much, the members also have to agree that the students should acquire the virtues, or dispositions, constituting the character of a moral agent.

According to the standards of moral agency, education has to help students become mature moral agents. It is to attain this goal by enabling them to develop the character of such agents. That character consists of cognitive and affective dispositions. The chief intellectual disposition is moral reasoning, which embodies the knowledge, skills, and appreciations needed for making choices and decisions consistent with the norms of moral agency. Other intellectual virtues might relate to science, technology, and aesthetics. The affective virtues are self-regarding and other-regarding. The former are such habits as hopefulness, moderation in pleasure, and self-esteem. The latter are such habits as empathy, charity, politeness, justice, and friendship. To be sure, education may have other aims, ranging from teaching handicapped students to master the ordinary skills of everyday life to teaching students to protect the environment or to prepare themselves for careers. Whatever the aims of education are, however, they must be compatible with that of enabling students to acquire the character of moral agents.

The content of education oriented to moral agency covers several areas: the commonplace world of the student, academic subjects, and career preparation. Because conditions in play, recreation, family relations, peer associations, community life, and the media significantly influence any individual's acquisition of freedom, knowledge, and the other features of moral agency, they have to be structured so that they will contribute to, not hinder, the moral character of students. In other words, families, neighborhoods, adolescent peer groups, churches, social agencies, and the media all have to tend to encourage the development of moral agency in children and other students. Because a school's academic curriculum that restricts the learning of moral agency to only one or a few subjects will tend to departmentalize and discount such agency, it must integrate that learning into all subject areas. Even in mathematics and natural science, which have concepts and methods applicable to judgments and deliberations by moral agents, there are ample opportunities for learning content important for the development of such agents. Because the services, products, and processes making up the world of commerce and art involve moral agents, they are subject to the norms of moral agency. Thus, the values, rules, and decisions specific to the utilitarian life must agree with the precepts of moral agency, and concern with the learning of moral character is appropriate to career preparation in these two areas.

Being moral agents, even if in different degrees, both teachers and students are subject to the standards of moral agency. Teachers logically value the purposefulness, evaluativeness, content, methods, and other factors involved in their teaching. They have the right to determine the specific habits to be acquired by their respective students and to choose the content and methods to be used in their teaching. Also, it is the moral duty of teachers not only to help their students develop as moral agents, but also to oppose hindrances to the growth of students as such agents. It hardly needs mentioning that teachers must exemplify to their students the characteristics of moral agency.

Students should become positively interested in the major features of moral agency. They have the right to the opportunity to acquire the character of a moral agent, to study whatever relevant subject matter appeals to themselves, to teaching that is appropriate to their ways of learning, and to the conditions that support and nurture the optimal development of their respective moral characters. As students grow in their capacity for moral action, they become increasingly responsible for respecting the rights of their teachers, one another, and other moral agents, and for maintaining and promoting the major traits of moral agency. Students have to acquire along the way those habits that enable them to develop as moral agents, for example, empathy, charity, self-denial, truthfulness, and a love of knowledge.

ASSESSMENT OF THE COMMITTEE MEMBERS' EDUCATIONAL VIEWS

Let us now consider to what extent the various educational views stated by the committee members are consistent with the values, rights, duties, and virtues of moral agency. On its surface, the minimal conception put forth by Mr. Schott and Mr. Jasper does not seem to violate any of these norms. For one thing, it appears to favor the rights and duties of interpersonal agency, for it allows that students need to learn to get along in society and that they need knowledge for living. Moreover, the conception expresses a disapproval of the loss of freedom in the county. The view arose from the perceptions by Mr. Schott and Mr. Jasper that the freedom of life choices for Biekman County's rural youth has significantly diminished with the decline in the agricultural sector of the county's economy.

Nevertheless, when we look below the surface, we detect some shortcomings in this minimal idea. One of them was identified by Ms. Reid, who insisted that the view treats the county's rural youth as passive and that it does not recognize that there are more life choices for these young people than farming and welfare. In other words, while the position of Mr. Schott and Mr. Jasper correctly regrets the loss of an estimable way of life, it fails to search for other life options so as to keep a relatively wide range of choices open for the county's rural youth. While Mr. Schott's objection that the nearby metropolitan job market was not suited to these young people was somewhat plausible, it regards them as uninterested in or incapable of developing their competencies so as to maintain or expand the range of choices open to themselves. When moral agents lose an option because of conditions beyond their control, they can maintain or increase their options only by altering the environment, altering themselves, or both. In the case of Biekman County's rural students, the more likely alternative is for them to try to gain competences that will enable them to enter new ways of life.

Another difficulty with the educational proposal suggested by Mr. Schott and Mr. Jasper relates to knowledge. The proposal in effect appreciates that basic academic knowledge is important for people to get by in Biekman County, and Mr. Schott also acknowledges that advanced knowledge is necessary for the better paying jobs in the metropolitan area. Yet, neither the proposal, Mr. Schott, nor Mr. Jasper recognizes the full value of knowledge for moral agency. Choices and decisions should be as well informed as they feasibly can be. Basic academic knowledge combined with common sense will enable a person to make some sound choices and some right decisions, but they are not likely to serve a person in judging and deliberating in the face of the complex and the unfamiliar. Confronted with these conditions, people may react impulsively or passively, but either way, they will lose control of their actions. According to Mr. Schott, at least, the children of Biekman County's farmers are not likely to be capable of or interested in acquiring advanced knowledge. But whether or not they are capable has to be determined by their performance in school. And whether or not they are interested depends upon whether or not their parents, their teachers, or other parties help them see the value of advanced knowledge in action. If the schools do not allow students to learn the knowledge of which they are capable, they violate the right that the students have to that knowledge. If schools do not teach students the full value of knowledge for moral action, they violate their duty to enable students to develop into mature moral agents.

In addition, the minimal conception suffers in its approach to the interpersonal aspect of moral action. While this idea recognizes that people in Biekman County are to interact with one another, it suggests a parochial bias about their interaction. It appears to presume that actions in the rural area will have little or no impact on those in Eldred and Flores and vice versa. Because it concerns only the education of students in the county's rural area, it suggests that what goes on there has little or nothing to do with what goes on in Flores and Eldred, such as higher taxes for higher welfare costs, and that what goes in those cities is not likely to have any impact in the rural area, such as increased traffic and real estate development. Moreover, the minimal proposal says nothing about helping the county's rural students to learn to interact with people from the diverse cultures in the local towns and cities let alone in the metropolitan area. Thus, instead of fostering respect, trust, politeness, and friendliness toward "outsiders," this proposal leaves an opening for disrespect, suspicion, and rudeness.

Let us now look at Ms. Spivak's optimal position, which holds that the Biekman County schools should help their students to do well in life. Because we do not know what Ms. Spivak intends by doing well in life or what she thinks the schools ought to do in helping students to this end, we cannot evaluate whatever it is she wants the schools to do. We can, nevertheless, relate her position to the norms of moral agency.

By our analysis of the concept of moral agency, we may infer that people do well in life only if what they do, whatever it is, agrees with the standards of moral agency. For instance, bankers do well in life only if they conduct their banking according to the norms of moral agency; artists do well only if they produce or perform according to those criteria. Because moral standards are superior to any other kind, the norms of moral agency imply that any standards with which they conflict are bad and thus unacceptable to moral agents. Even though following the standards of moral agency is doing well as a moral agent, it alone does not ensure doing well completely in life. The reason, quite simply, is that there are many kinds of norms in life other than that of moral agency. There are standards of communication, business, art, love, science, politics, spying, gambling, engineering, warfare, crafts, athletics, leisure, and so on. While a person might always be morally true, he or she might do poorly in business, art, love, science, or some other field. It is maintained, then, that whatever Ms. Spivak means by doing well in life, she should intend that it will be consistent with the criteria of moral agency. So, if she is serious about Biekman County's schools enabling their students to do well in life, she apparently wants the schools to help their students develop according to the norms of moral agency as well as learn other kinds of standards that will apply to different areas of life in which the students are likely to participate.

While the other types of standards Ms. Spivak wants the students to learn are not clear, likely candidates come to mind: criteria of academic performance, career principles, rules of conduct, and rules of citizenship. But what about the criteria of parenting, nutrition, love, and coping with death? We cannot assume that she does or does not want these included. Indeed, one wonders what reasons she would have for including or excluding the standards of some area of life. To resolve this issue, we should consider three things. First, we ought to consider which institutions in Biekman County other than schools are effectively educating the county's youth in kinds of norms that agree with those of moral agency. After all, schools should neither duplicate nor interfere with the desirable operations of other institutions. Second, we should consider which of the county's institutions are ineffectively educating the county's youth in norms consistent with moral agency. The schools might do well by supplementing the work of these institutions. Third, we ought to consider if any institutions are inculcating norms opposed to those of moral agency. Do families or television programs, for instance, definitely promote violence, selfishness, hedonism, racism, drug addiction, irresponsibility, or irrationality? If there are such institutions, the schools might not have sufficient authority to correct them. But they might be able to obtain help from other agencies for constructing and implementing programs that will counteract the influence of those institutions.

Some of our discussion of Ms. Spivak's position bears upon Mr. Gibbs's proposal for school programs that will help prepare students for their chosen careers. Whether a career is in banking, art, agriculture, social work, or some other area, it is norm governed. Being inferior to moral standards, those norms governing an occupation are worthy or unworthy for moral agents according to the criteria of moral agency. In his call for career preparation, Mr. Gibbs probably has in mind programs that help students learn academic knowledge and skills presupposed by occupations of interest, learn to follow rules of conduct and citizenship supportive of such careers, and learn to act according to the norms special to the occupations of their respective choices. Quite likely, it has not occurred to Mr. Gibbs that all of these various kinds of standards, including those special to careers, should agree with those of moral agency. But it will not do for schools anywhere to offer career-oriented programs without ensuring that the principles taught in those programs are consistent with being a moral agent. Indeed, it is arguable that such programs should emphasize the restraints of moral agency upon careers. A career should not mean striving for success at any cost. It ought not to mean deceiving customers and clients. It should not mean a disregard of the price and quality of products and services. It should not mean neglect of employees. It should not mean that men have careers and women have odd jobs and housework. Nor should it mean anything else opposed to the values, rights, duties, and virtues of moral agency.

Another critical point about Mr. Gibbs's idea pertains to its presumption that one's ambition for an occupation should be the organizing principle of the education offered at Biekman County's schools. To be sure, a career might be the center of a person's life. Whom a person marries, where one lives, the time spent with one's family, the church that one attends, the clothes that one wears, the recreation that one pursues—these and other matters are sometimes dependent upon a person's vocation. In truth, people whose jobs are divorced from the rest of their lives are often said to be unfortunate, to be alienated from their work. Yet, while Mr. Gibbs seems justified in holding that education ordered around vocational ambitions might be of much value to the students of Biekman County, he also fails to recognize that such an education might run counter to the knowledge and freedom associated with moral agency.

More specifically, he does not see that his proposed education might not provide students with knowledge that they presently or will need for making informed choices and decisions in some areas of their lives and that it might restrict their freedom to make life choices and decisions. The knowledge supportive of an occupational choice might not be relevant to some sectors of life. Suppose that a student chooses to be a welder or a lawyer. What knowledge leading to either career will help that student make judgments and decisions relevant to being a good parent or neighbor or understand art? In addition, to focus the education of students on the career ambitions that they have in school is likely to hinder or at least not encourage their freedom to make changes in their career goals later. It is Mr. Gibbs who, ironically, complains that school students are fickle in their interests. Hence, he should at least entertain the possibility that they will alter their career goals after leaving school. Also, according to policy experts, members of the rising generation of Americans must be prepared to change careers several times during their working lives. Superintendent Moore, who anticipates alterations in the economic conditions of Biekman County in the foreseeable future, supposedly would agree that this recommendation applies especially to that county's students. Hence, if education at Biekman County's schools were to center around student career ambitions, it would not assist them in making the new career choices that they presumably would want to make after leaving school. Moreover, because that education likely would give students the impression that they need not consider making new vocational choices as economic circumstances alter, it would encourage the county's students to be passive in the face of such circumstances.

The concerns about student behavior that are expressed by Reverend Johnson, Ms. Reid, Ms. Fowler, and Mr. Gibbs contain two difficulties. One is that the moral principles lying behind their concerns are not clear. Are they essentially religious? If so, are they completely justifiable by good reasons or do they ultimately rest on faith? Can they be taught in public schools without violation of the First Amendment of the United States Constitution? Finally, do they concord with the norms of moral agency? In view of the committee members' more or less positive interest in freedom, one may infer that their moral beliefs have at least some agreement with the criteria of moral agency. Nevertheless, because the members have not fully explained their position on freedom or any other features of moral agency that they might favor, they provide no evidence of how substantial that agreement is.

The other problem relates to the sources of the student misbehavior. Through references to family conditions and to television programs, Reverend Johnson indicates that the troubled behavior of the county's youth originates with factors beyond classrooms and school grounds. Mr. Gibbs, too, seems to support this view. Nevertheless, all committee members appear to hold that their schools can do something, in both the short and the long run, that will tend to improve student behavior. Ms. Fowler, for instance, believes that students will behave themselves in the classroom if teachers make their subjects interesting to them. Ms. Reid suggests that programs in sex education and parenting will help. While these possible measures are worth exploring, they might not be effective by themselves. After all, if student misbehavior is caused by factors beyond the schools, it might not be correctible by actions undertaken by the schools alone. It is possible, even likely, that the policies suggested by the committee members will be successful only if they are tied to measures designed to alter community attitudes toward schooling, familial relationships, television viewing, and other non-school matters in Biekman County. While the schools probably do not have sufficient authority to initiate and implement such extensive measures completely, they can work with other agencies on measures of this kind.

We should not dismiss the committee members' concern with school costs, school taxes, and the county's economy as irrelevant to moral agency. That recommendations on these matters are not appropriate to the mission of the county's schools does not mean that they are unimportant for the mission. Schools, which cannot function without personnel and material resources, must have the economic support necessary for fulfilling their mission. If, therefore, the schools of Biekman County are to educate their students within the framework of the norms of moral agency, they have to have the economic support that will enable them to do their job. Taxes dedicated to that end will be justifiable for moral as well as educational reasons. Efforts to enhance the tax base of Biekman County will be justifiable for the same kinds of reasons.

How much tax the county's school system may levy is also of moral concern. Because immature moral agents have a right to development as moral agents, they may demand, through proxies, assistance from mature moral agents to attain that development. Thus, the youth of Biekman County have a right as moral agents to financial assistance from the county's adults for an education governed by the standards of moral agency. Nevertheless, no moral agent has a right to support something that would pose a morally inordinate burden upon others. For instance, the assistance should not deprive the providers of what they physically need to function as moral agents. So, while the property owners of Biekman County arguably should pay taxes to support schooling consistent with the norms of moral agency, they should not have to pay taxes at a rate that will impoverish them. Mr. Gibbs was morally right, then, in holding that school expenses should not be more than the citizens of the county can bear.

TOWARD A MISSION STATEMENT

Our critique of the discussion by the Mission Statement Committee has been largely negative to this point. Despite having mentioned several strengths of the various educational proposals presented by committee members, the evaluation has devoted most of its effort to identifying weaknesses. Embedded in the critique, however, are guidelines for the committee members to follow in revising their ideas. These guidelines do not specify a mission statement for the members, but they direct them toward a statement that will give the schools of Biekman County a mission that reflects the norms of moral agency.

Guideline No. 1: All the students of Biekman County need the opportunity to learn advanced academic knowledge. This guideline, referring to the importance of knowledge for moral agency, is in response to our criticism of the minimal proposal set forth by Mr. Schott and Mr. Jasper. It is to ensure that all students have equal opportunity to learn to make informed choices and decisions in a world of rapid change, great complexity, and high technology.

Guideline No. 2: The schools of Biekman County should help all their students to expand their horizons of life choices. This advisory, which reflects the value of freedom for moral agents, originated in Ms. Spivak's complaint that the proposal by Mr. Schott and Mr. Jasper presumes a very narrow range of life choices for the county's rural students. Nevertheless, the guideline is applicable to Ms. Fowler's recommendation that teachers make their classes interesting to students. Students may pursue interests or develop them. If they develop their interests, they are more likely to expand their horizons of choice, but if they merely pursue them, they are less likely. Thus, when teachers endeavor to make their classes interesting, they must ensure that they enable their students to develop, not just pursue, their interests.

Guideline No. 3: The schools ought to enable all students to be receptive to interpersonal relations with moral agents regardless of the latter's racial, cultural, and geographic characteristics. Reflecting the interpersonal relations involved in moral agency, this recommendation derives from our concern about the localism that seemed to tint the minimal position.

Guideline No. 4: The schools ought not to organize their programs around specific career choices. Springing from our examination of Mr. Gibbs's proposal for the county's schools to educate students according to their career ambitions, this advisory expresses our concern that the students of Biekman County not only are likely to change their career goals after leaving school but will probably need to learn to change careers several times during their working lives. It also reflects the point that there is more to life than a vocation. It does not preclude career preparation entirely; it simply speaks against educational programs that simply prepare students for specific jobs. It allows for the teaching of concept formation, critical thinking, problem solving, and other higher order thinking skills along with job training, but it also allows for teaching such skills without job training.

Guideline No. 5: The schools need to ensure that whatever is taught to their students is consistent with the norms of moral agency. This directive applies not only to academic subjects but also to occupational studies and to morality. Even though the Mission Statement Committee members do not reveal the extent to which they are open to the principles of moral agency, they do indicate that they have some committment to knowledge, freedom, and interpersonal relations. Even if they rest that committment on a bedrock of religious faith, they could go along with the norms of moral agency without agreeing to their rationalistic basis.

Guideline No. 6: The Biekman County Unified School System has to cooperate with community groups and other county agencies in controlling social factors that influence the behavior of students but are beyond the control of just that system. Thus, the system's administrators, teachers, and board members have to recognize that their programs cannot be exclusively of their making. At least some of their educational programs have to emerge from interaction among various elements of the county's social structure. Superintendent Moore, then, will have to work with other leaders not only in strengthening the county's tax base but also in dealing with some of the county's social problems.

4

School Justice

Student misconduct in America's public schools has been of serious concern in recent decades. While teachers and administrators recognize that student behavior generally is imperfect, they have encountered a marked increase in student criminal activity, for instance, drug trafficking, rape, and possession and use of weapons. Thus, teachers and administrators have found themselves diverting time and energy from helping students learn academic subjects to trying to control their conduct. They also have discovered that the misbehavior has tended to contaminate the educational climate of schools. Teachers and administrators, of course, are not the only ones who have been disturbed by this surge in misconduct. Parents have complained about the lack of safety for their children and the disruption of classroom learning. Politicians and others have pointed to the increase as one more sign of the failure of the nation's public schools. Social scientists have spoken of the misbehavior as indicative of an anomie that is likely to be embedded in a sizable portion of American young people for the foreseeable future. The federal government has adopted recommendations to make the nation's schools safe, disciplined, and drug free.

In efforts to reduce this lack of discipline, public school leaders have designed and implemented a variety of preventive measures: the banishment of culprits and "trouble makers" to alternative schools, chain-link fencing with highly restricted access, security officers, surveillance cameras, hall patrols by teachers, on-campus police arrests of student members of gangs, community concern programs, locker searches, student informants, restriction of the time and area of student movement, employment of metal detectors when searching students for weapons, and the banning of student possession and use of "beepers" and other electronic communication devices. To inform students of these and other measures, public school leaders have taken steps to update their student conduct codes.

But it is one thing to try to prevent criminal activity in any manner and quite another to do so in a just way. While justice in the United States demands that the government, whether federal, state, or local, shall protect the innocent and the public good, it requires also that in protecting them the government shall not violate the rights of any person, including any suspect or convicted person. Not only must the government take care to convict and punish only the guilty but also its laws must not threaten anybody's rights, and its investigations must follow procedures that do not threaten anybody's rights. Because our public schools and their teachers and administrators are governmental agencies and agents, they are bound by these guidelines of justice. Accordingly, the demands of American justice also have diverted time and energy from the business of educating students.

THE SITUATION AT FLOWERS MIDDLE SCHOOL

Flowers Middle School has a student body about evenly divided between white and black students. The white students typically are economically well off while the black students generally are not. The school's curriculum is strong in extracurricular activities as well as academics, and student performance in both sectors is fairly good on the whole. Parental support of the school is unmistakably apparent by the large turnouts at the school's parents' nights and at its band concerts. Maintaining discipline at the school has been relatively easy. The vast majority of the students get along well, and they usually respect their teachers' admonitions. Lately, however, several incidents have indicated that keeping discipline might become difficult. During the past semester, several fights occurred in the school cafeteria, where none had taken place before. Some students, both boys and girls, complained of being physically abused in restrooms by other students.

A few girls yelled at their teachers, and several boys were found with knives in their possession.

Ms. Barbara Williams has been principal of Flowers Middle School for two years. She has solid academic credentials, and she has a splendid reputation for her past work at other schools, both as a teacher and as an assistant principal. After taking the leadership position at Flowers, she quickly gained the support of her faculty and of parents. That support had little to do with her being the first African American to be principal of the school. Rather, it derived mainly from her effectiveness in continuing the school's academic and extracurricular programs and from her commitment to maintain the school's healthy learning climate. Indeed, since noting last semester's increase in disciplinary cases, she has become even more determined to protect that climate.

Flowers certainly is not the only school in the district to suffer a growth in disciplinary problems. Rude speech by students to teachers has become frequent in the high schools. The enforcement of dress codes in all high schools has been hopeless for some time. The cost of damage to restrooms in some schools has started to exceed budget projections. Three schools have had bomb scares. Several dozen students have been arrested for possession and distribution of drugs. In addition, weapons have become an especially disturbing matter. A fifth grade student displayed a loaded pistol on the playground. Several years ago dozens of knives each semester were found through searches. A few student members of opposing gangs have engaged in fights in which injuries have been inflicted with knives and sharpened screw drivers. Also, there have been gang-related shootings in the neighborhoods of two schools.

To curb and reduce the possession of weapons at school, the superintendent of the district, Thomas Delmar, had a weapons policy drafted by an assistant and approved by the district board of education. It reads in its entirety: "Any student with any weapon on school grounds or elsewhere during a school activity will be expelled from his or her school for a period equivalent to two school semesters and enrolled during that period in the district's alternative school." The superintendent told all his principals that he expected all of them to enforce the policy strictly and vigorously. He also ordered them to announce the rule to all students and to have their parents or guardians sign and return copies of it.

THE CASE OF RICHARD DOBBINS

Richard Dobbins is in the seventh grade at Flowers Middle School. In capability he is above average; in motivation he is about average. His father manages a thriving insurance agency, and his mother works as a legal secretary. While the Dobbinses do not dote on Richard, who is their only child, they are prepared to furnish him with any opportunity he might need to have a successful life. They would be very pleased if he would enter the field of law or medicine, but they have never pushed him in any direction. They believe that if they provide him with a good home environment and a good education, he eventually will make a career choice with which they all will be pleased. They and Richard get along well, and they find that Flowers provides him with a variety of worthy academic and social opportunities. They accept the fact that their son presently shows little or no interest in thinking about a career path. Indeed, they have only one worry about him: This school year he has seemed to be somewhat uncomfortable in relating to his teachers and most of his classmates. During last month's parents' night, two teachers mentioned to Richard's parents that while their son paid attention and did satisfactory work, he chose to sit apart from the other students. The parents have assumed, however, that this is a developmental problem, one that will go away with time.

So, it was with shock that Mr. and Mrs. Dobbins read the letter that they received from Ms. Williams. In the letter, Ms. Williams said that she was recommending severe disciplinary action against Richard. He had a knife in his possession during a recent science class excursion and that, according to regulations, he was liable to be expelled from Flowers Middle School for a period of two semesters and enrolled for that period in the school district's alternative school. The letter mentioned further that should the parents wish to appeal this recommendation, they should notify the superintendent's office within ten days. Until a disposition of an appeal is known, the letter concluded, Richard would be removed from his regular classes and placed in the "time out" program at Flowers Middle School.

Mr. and Mrs. Dobbins quickly consulted with Richard on what had happened. The thrust of his terse and subdued answers was that he in fact was found with a knife when he went with his class to the science museum. It was the pocket knife given to him on his last birthday by his grandfather. While the parents agreed that Richard should not escape punishment for his violation of school rules, they believed that a two-semester expulsion was entirely indefensible and that an appeals hearing at the superintendent's office was unnecessary. They concluded that they should obtain an appointment with Ms. Williams and work out with her an appropriate plan immediately. The next morning, Mr. and Mrs. Dobbins received their second shock when they learned from Ms. Williams that she could not talk with them about Richard's case for it now was totally in the hands of the superintendent's office. If they wished to discuss the case, they could do so only during an appeals hearing. While somewhat dismayed, they managed to get a hearing arranged for the following week. During the next few days, Mrs. Dobbins was able to discuss the family's situation with the attorney for whom she worked. He explained that schools have some leeway in their disciplinary policies and that they have to respect a student's rights under the laws of the United States and their state. He also suggested a few points that might be in Richard's favor.

The site for the appeal is a large conference room in the building occupied by the district's department of education. On one side of the large table sit Ms. Williams and a school security officer dressed in sport coat and slacks. On the other side sit Mr. and Mrs. Dobbins and Richard. Dr. Janice Cooper, an associate superintendent, is chair of the meeting. On the table there is a microphone for taping the discussion.

Dr. Cooper: I wish to explain our procedures to you. This is not a court of law, but we have to have a reasonable way for both parties to communicate with one another. The microphone is there so that I can record our discussion. I will open the discussion by reading the charge against Richard. Then Mr. and Mrs. Dobbins may present whatever objections they have. Ms. Williams, the principal of Flowers Middle School, is here as a witness to the charge against Richard. Mr. Jackson, who is a school district security officer, is here as a witness to Richard's conduct. Mr. and Mrs. Dobbins, you may ask questions of Ms. Williams and Mr. Jackson if you so desire. After this hearing is over, I will return to my office with the tapes and my notes. Within about a week, I will notify all parties of my decision. Does anyone have any concerns to express before we begin? Seeing that there are none, I will read the charge.

"Two weeks ago, on March 16, Richard Dobbins went on a school bus with the rest of his science class to the municipal science museum. While the students were sitting on the bus and waiting to enter the museum, one of them saw Richard with a knife scratching the paint on the seat frame in front of him. That student reported the incident to the science teacher, who in turn informed Mr. Jackson, a school security officer accompanying the group on their trip. After all the other students had left the bus with their teacher, Mr. Jackson searched Richard and found a pocket knife on him. Mr. Jackson later reported his finding to Ms. Williams. According to school district procedure, Ms. Williams promptly turned the case over to the superintendent's office for disposition and also notified Mr. and Mrs. Dobbins of the matter.

"This school district has a policy strictly banning the possession of weapons by students on school grounds and anywhere else during a school activity. This policy makes expulsion for a period equivalent to two semesters the punishment for such possession. It allows no exceptions. Richard Dobbins has been determined to have violated the policy in that he possessed a pocket knife on a school bus during a school excursion. Therefore, he must be expelled from Flowers Middle School and enrolled in the alternative school for a total of two school semesters."

Mr. and Mrs. Dobbins, I have finished with the charge. You now may state your objections.

Mr. Dobbins: Well, Dr. Cooper, it is almost impossible for us to give any objections at this time since this is the first time that we have been informed of the exact charge. Ms. Williams's letter told us that Richard was accused of having a knife, but it said nothing about the circumstances. May we postpone this hearing until we have had time to study the written charge and make our objections on the basis of it?

Dr. Cooper: I am sorry, Mr. Dobbins, but I see no reason to do that. It would cause useless delay. Your letter from Ms. Williams gave you the substance of the charge, and I do not believe that the exact wording of the charge should make any difference in what your objections might be. Moreover, we have the people here who can answer any questions you might have about the charge. So, you might want to ask Ms. Williams or Mr. Jackson about matters that are not clear to you yet. There is plenty of time this morning to get things straightened out.

Mr. Dobbins: Okay, but we'll have to take some time to figure out a few things before we can know just what objections are relevant. I believe that you have on the table the knife that Richard is supposed to have had on the bus. May I look at the knife, please? Thank you, Dr. Cooper. Now, Richard, is this your knife?

Richard: Yes, sir. It's the one that Grandpa gave me.

Mr. Dobbins: Did Mr. Jackson search you on the bus and find the knife on you?

Richard: Yes, sir.

Mr. Dobbins: Mr. Jackson, why did you search Richard?

Mr. Jackson: Because Richard's teacher told me that he had been seen with a knife.

Mr. Dobbins: Ms. Williams, who saw Richard with the knife?

Ms. Williams: One of Richard's classmates. I have the name some place in my file here.

Mr. Dobbins: Is that student available for this meeting?

Dr. Cooper: No, she is not. We normally do not have student witnesses miss school for this kind of meeting.

Mr. Dobbins: I am not trying to be difficult, Dr. Cooper. But I cannot be sure that Richard was lawfully searched unless I have a chance to talk with that student. There is no doubt that Richard had this knife on him and that it was found by Mr. Jackson. But I am not certain that Mr. Jackson had the right to search Richard. What if the student had lied or fantasized about seeing Richard with the knife? What if the teacher believed that student without even double checking? What if somebody was out to get Richard? Is the teacher available for this meeting?

Dr. Cooper: No, he is not. He has classes to teach.

Mr. Dobbins: Well, I now wish to state an objection that Mrs. Dobbins and I have: We think that the search of Richard might have violated his right against an unreasonable search. Until we have had a chance to interview the student witness and the teacher, we cannot believe that Richard's right was not violated. Mrs. Dobbins, I believe, has some questions now.

Dr. Cooper: Go ahead, Mrs. Dobbins.

Mrs. Dobbins: Richard, is this the first time you ever had your knife at school?

Richard: Yes, ma'm.

Mrs. Dobbins: Did you take it on the trip so that you could hurt somebody?

Richard: No, ma'm.

Ms. Williams: May I say something here, please?

Mrs. Dobbins: Surely.

Ms. Williams: One or two students told me they had heard that Richard was seen at his locker with the knife on other days.

Mr. Dobbins: Ms. Williams, if I may interrupt. I am no lawyer, but that sounds like hearsay evidence. Those students just heard about something; they did not see it themselves. I do not think such evidence should be considered here.

Dr. Cooper: I agree, Mr. Dobbins. Mrs. Dobbins, would you please continue.

Mrs. Dobbins: Thank you. Ms. Williams, does Richard have any other case of misconduct entered into his record at your school?

Ms. Williams: No, he does not. Until now, he has followed the rules quite well.

Mrs. Dobbins: Then, my husband and I wish to give our next objection: You are treating Richard without considering the circumstances of what Richard did and without considering his life of good conduct. He was not threatening anybody with the knife and had no intention to do so. That he broke the rules this one time means only that he is a human, not a criminal.

Dr. Cooper: Let me try to explain something at this point if I may, Mrs. Dobbins. The rule that Richard broke is very plain: It says that any student with any weapon on school grounds or during a school activity elsewhere will be expelled for two academic semesters. It allows no exceptions for first-time offenders or for a history of good conduct.

Mrs. Dobbins: Dr. Cooper, are you saying that if the very best student in your district violated that rule just once in a harmless way, he or she would be expelled and placed in the alternative school for a year?

Dr. Cooper: Yes, that is what I am saying, and I can assure you that dozens of students have been found to have violated our weapons policy and no exceptions have been made.

Mrs. Dobbins: I suppose, then, that my husband and I want to state another objection, which, I believe, will be our third. This one is that your weapons policy is harsh; it is like the laws of ancient times. I have never heard of an American law that did not take into account a person's intentions, whether or not a violation was a person's first, and whether or not the person had a record of good behavior. I do not know if this policy is unusual for schools, but being a mother, I can say that it is a cruel policy.

Dr. Cooper: Thank you, Mrs. Dobbins. I have recorded your third objection. Are there others?

Mr. Dobbins: Well, I might have one, depending on the answer to a question. Dr. Cooper, what is the purpose of the weapons rule?

Dr. Cooper: A good question. The purpose is to eliminate weapons from the schools. You may not be aware of it, Mr. Dobbins, but several years ago our schools were looking at a serious weapons problem.

Dozens of students were carrying them and not just knives. Several students were injured by them. Armed gangs in the neighborhoods of a couple of schools had members in the schools. We had to do something to stop this problem, so the district approved the weapons policy. Since implementing the policy, the district has had a definite reduction in the number of weapons incidents.

Mr. Dobbins: But I do not see how expelling students will keep them from carrying weapons. It might scare some students already behaving themselves, but it won't stop a person already prone to carrying a weapon. Won't it just put most of the armed students in the alternative school?

Dr. Cooper: That's the idea, Mr. Dobbins. By having those students in the same school, we can keep a closer watch on them. In fact, we have regular searches and that way keep weapons out of that school.

Mr. Dobbins: You mean that if Richard went to the alternative school, he would be regularly searched so as to keep him from bringing a weapon there?

Dr. Cooper: Yes, sir, he would be treated like all the other students.

Mr. Dobbins: But what does the alternative school do for its students other than keep them from carrying weapons and, I suppose, using alcohol and drugs? I read in the newspaper this past year that a little more than half of its students wind up in the youth detention center. Is that true?

Dr. Cooper: I do not know what the exact figures are. But I do remember reading the report to which you are referring and agreeing that its numbers seemed approximately right.

Mr. Dobbins: That article also said that more than half of those in the youth detention center eventually go to prison. So, I just can't see that the alternative school is doing much for its students, and I certainly can't see that it can possibly contribute to Richard's education.

Dr. Cooper: Now, Mr. Dobbins, you should understand that the alternative school is accredited and that Richard will have a study program planned according to his needs.

Mr. Dobbins: That is not my point, Dr. Wilson. At best, the climate of that school will upset Richard where he cannot concentrate on his studies. It might even terrorize him. It is also possible, of course, that Richard will learn how to carry weapons without detection and even how to use drugs. Mrs. Dobbins and myself, therefore, have a fourth objection, which is that the punishment you have recommended for Richard is entirely wrong. I am not saying that Richard should be excused from any punishment for what he has done, but I am saying that putting him in that alternative school for a year is not even close to being appropriate.

Dr. Cooper: I have noted your latest objection here. Do you or Mrs. Dobbins have any others to present? No? Then, I want to take this opportunity to summarize your four objections:

1. Richard Dobbins might not have been lawfully searched.
2. The circumstances of Richard's act and Richard's history of behavior were not considered.
3. The weapons policy is harsh; it does not allow for differences among acts and violators.
4. The punishment prescribed for Richard under the weapons policy is inappropriate.

These are the objections as I understand them. Mr. and Mrs. Dobbins, have I stated them as you mean them? Okay, then as I explained at the outset, I will study the record of this hearing and let all parties know my decision, I hope, in another week. I thank each of you for your cooperation.

Driving home from the meeting, Mr. and Mrs. Dobbins allowed that the meeting had been worthwhile. They had made some points which, they thought, Dr. Cooper and Ms. Williams appeared to appreciate. After a few more comments about the hearing, Mrs. Dobbins asked Richard, who was sitting in the back seat, why he took the knife out of his pocket while he was on the bus and why he was scratching the paint on the seat frame. He looked impassively out the window next to him and said, very quitely: "I don't know; I knew it was wrong. I just felt like it. I just wanted to do it, I guess." The rest of the drive home passed in silence.

Ten days later, Ms. Williams opened Dr. Cooper's letter to her and the Dobbinses. The main passage of the letter appeared in the middle paragraph: "Having reviewed the evidence and the objections presented at the hearing, I have found that Richard Dobbins did violate the school district's weapons policy and that, according to that policy, he must be immediately expelled from Flowers Middle School. However, I also have decided that Richard should not serve the full punishment dictated by the weapons policy. He is to be enrolled in the alternative school, pending good conduct, for only the remainder of this semester." The letter concluded by mentioning that any appeal of this decision must be presented to the district's board of education. Upon finishing the letter, Ms. Williams felt relieved that she received support in enforcing the weapons policy against Richard but relieved also that he had received a notably reduced punishment. She thought that nobody with Richard's conduct record and character needed two semesters in the alternative school.

Mr. and Mrs. Dobbins pondered whether or not to appeal Dr. Cooper's decision. While they were pleased that she had taken their objections seriously, they were not sure that Richard should be in the alternative school for even half of a semester. On the other hand, they had no way of knowing if the school board would be receptive to their views. Maybe a prolonged appeals process might simply distract Richard from his studies. Maybe they should settle for Dr. Cooper's decision so that Richard could get this bad experience behind him this semester and then get on with his education next fall. They presumed that he could survive a couple of months at the alternative school without suffering any lasting harm.

IDENTIFICATION OF THE CENTRAL TOPIC

Now let us analyze the case of Richard Dobbins within the framework of moral agency. To do this, we will focus upon a pervasive topic, or theme, in the case. It will be recalled that our first task when discussing the meeting of the Mission Statement Committee of the Biekman County Unified School District was to settle upon a dominant topic, which was education. That step enabled us to organize our analysis around the topic of education.

Throughout the Richard Dobbins case there is a concern with justice of some kind. Since ancient times, philosophers have distinguished several kinds of justice. Retributive justice concerns punishment for the violation of a rule. Compensatory justice pertains to making amends for harm done to a person. Distributive justice relates to the distribution of goods and services, and procedural justice concerns the procedures followed in an investigation, trial, or hearing. The justice immediately at stake in Richard's case is neither compensatory nor distributive. No party at the hearing is seeking compensation for some harm done, and no one is definitely interested in whether or not some person received a fair share of certain goods or services. The justice of direct relevance to the case is retributive and procedural. No one doubts that Richard broke the weapons rule; in addition, no one holds that Richard should not be punished. But there is contention between the school officials and Richard's parents about what is a fair penalty for Richard: the one set forth in the weapons policy or the one tempered by the circumstances of Richard's errant behavior and the otherwise unblemished record of his conduct. Procedural justice in the case bears on procedures followed during the appeals meeting and during the gathering of evidence. Mr. Dobbins opened his discussion by commenting on the procedure of having to make objections to the formal charge against Richard without having previously known of its specific content. He posed another question of procedural justice when he maintained that Mr. Jackson might not have had a legitimate cause to search Richard. Also, he raised a procedural issue by insisting that the hearsay evidence presented by Ms. Williams ought to be excluded from the meeting.

Questions about fairness in punishment and about procedural justice are familiar to any person who has watched the fictional and the real courtroom dramas broadcast by television. Yet, even though they are stock items in judicial proceedings, they are not exclusively judicial issues. After all, as Dr. Cooper cautions, the appeals meeting is not a court hearing. It is, nevertheless, a legal hearing. To be sure, the weapons policy discussed at that meeting is not a constitutional law or a statute, that is, a law created by a legislature. It is, rather, an administrative law, or a rule enacted by an institution (in Richard's case, the public school district of concern) to facilitate its operation. Constitutional and statutory laws apply to all members of a given public, whereas an administrative rule applies only to those under the aegis of the relevant institution. The hearing, then, is administrative. Administrative laws and hearings, however, stand in the shadow of constitutional and statutory laws, for as Mrs. Dobbins's employer, the attorney, explained, the former may not oppose the latter in certain respects.

But we should recognize that in Richard's case the issues about punishment and procedures are more than administrative and judicial; they also are moral. All the parties to the case are moral beings. Richard, of course, is not morally mature, but he presumably was largely informed of what he was doing and presumably did it freely. Moreover, his act directly or indirectly influenced other people, ranging from other students to Mr. Jackson, Ms. Williams, his parents, Dr. Cooper, and perhaps his grandfather. So, while on one level the appeals hearing is an administrative hearing concerned with behavior detrimental to the functioning of certain public schools, it is on a deeper level a discussion among moral beings concerned with a wrong act by one of their number. Hence, the question of fairness in punishment is not just a question of what is fair punishment for a member of an institution who has broken a certain rule of that institution. It is, in addition, an issue of what is fair punishment for an immature moral being who has violated that rule. It is this issue that requires a consideration of the moral qualities, rights, and duties of the student, as well as a consideration of the moral justification of the rule. A similar point may be made about the issue of procedural justice. At its moral level, this is a question of what are the procedures needed to ensure that all parties of the appeals hearing will be fully informed of the facts of Richard's case and of the moral values, rights, and duties at stake in the case.

A few of the people mentioned in connection with Richard's case speak of at least some of the distinctions just drawn. Both Dr. Cooper and the attorney employing Mrs. Dobbins refer to the appeals hearing as being different from a judicial hearing. Ms. Williams seems to view the hearing as mainly concerned with a school affair. Also, Superintendent Delmar presumably regards the weapons policy as an administrative, not a statutory, rule and any appeals hearing on any case falling under the policy as an administrative, rather than a judicial, matter. Richard's parents, as well as Dr. Cooper, appear to hold, somewhat dimly, the concept of procedural fairness. Perhaps Mrs. Dobbins picked up the distinction from her employer; perhaps Mr. Dobbins picked it up in the course of his insurance work, which might have involved some judicial inquiries.

That any person related to the case consciously views it as one of morality is problematic. While Dr. Cooper might have decided to reduce Richard's punishment because of a sense of what is morally appropriate, she also might have done so for purely administrative reasons. Institutional justice would allow the reduced punishment simply because Richard poses no serious threat to the order of the schools and because his reduced punishment would maintain at least a semblance of following the weapons policy. Even though Richard's parents might be acting partly from a moral standpoint, they seem to be acting mainly from what is good for Richard. Mr. Dobbins does wonder whether the alternative school has value for any of its students, but he and Mrs. Dobbins seem focused primarily upon their son's education and future life. In other words, their concerns seem mainly prudential, not moral. Thus, one suspects that their insistence upon a fair punishment for Richard and upon procedural fairness is motivated not so much by an interest in Richard's development as a moral being as by an interest in his opportunity to have a prosperous and happy life.

Ms. Williams has something quite like a moral concern. To be sure, she also has an administrative viewpoint. The weapons policy is a school rule, and as a diligent school official, she enforces it. But we learn, from the relief she felt upon learning about Richard's reduced punishment, that she was silently troubled by the prospect of his having to attend the alternative school for two semesters. Clearly, this is not an administrative concern, for she is not worrying simply whether or not the reduced sentence is commensurate with the smooth functioning of the schools. It is not a prudential matter either, for it is based on her idea of what might be beneficial for anybody with Richard's conduct record and character. While Ms. Williams's conscientious feeling is not an articulate moral concern, it can be easily transformed into one through reflection and discussion.

THE FEATURES OF MORAL AGENCY

Having identified justice as a topic pervading the case of Richard Dobbins and having determined the various notions of justice related to the case, we want to raise the question of what justice should be in the case. But before we take up that question, we need to ask this: By what criteria will we judge that a claim of justice in the case is defensible? The criteria ultimately have to be moral ones. Because moral principles are superior to all others, moral standards of justice will enable us to pass judgment upon all other kinds, including judicial, statutory, and administrative. Moral norms of justice, we believe, lie within the framework of moral agency. To specify those norms and relate them to Richard's case, we have to show in what respects the features and major norms of moral agency are relevant to the case.

Knowledge

Without doubt, knowledge is a feature of moral agency reflected by the Richard Dobbins case. It shows up when Superintendent Delmar insists that all students and their parents are to be informed of the weapons policy. It is present in Mr. Dobbins's request to have a delay of the hearing so that he and Mrs. Dobbins may have time to study the formal charges against Richard. It pertains to the discussion of evidence about what Richard did, including the dispute over whether or not hearsay should count as evidence and whether or not Mr. Jackson's discovery of the knife on Richard should count as evidence. It bears on the availability of the student and the teacher witnesses for questioning. It appears in Mr. Dobbins's recitation of statistics about former students of the alternative school. Also, it is significant for Richard's state of mind. That Richard admitted to scratching the paint with the knife, said that he did not intend to hurt anyone with the knife, and stated that he knew at the time his behavior was wrong indicate that he was fairly knowledgeable of his action. But that he could not or chose not to explain fully why he committed the act suggests that he might not have been acting in full knowledge.

Freedom

Freedom is another characteristic of moral agency that figures in the case. As far as we can tell, all of the adults connected with the case acted freely. While Ms. Williams had to discipline Richard, she *had to* not in the sense that she was compelled to but in the sense that she was obligated to. While Mr. and Mrs. Dobbins acted as parents in appealing Ms. Williams's decision, they were acting by choice rather than under the force of some parental instinct. While all parties at the hearing followed procedural rules, they were not necessarily acting unfreely for following them. Without rules, they would have had chaos, not freedom.

Richard's freedom, however, is somewhat problematic. Nobody forced him to take the knife to school or to use it on the bus. Moreover, there is nothing in his cultural background that drove him to violate the weapons policy. Yet, there are two facts that cause us to wonder if he was in complete control of his action. One fact is that he could not explain why he scratched the paint with the knife beyond saying that he just felt like doing it. The other fact is that he had chosen to sit apart from the other students during class. To be sure, he could have acted on impulse, that is, just because he felt like scratching the paint with his knife. But that account leads to the question of why he brought the knife to school in the first place. Why would he risk getting into serious trouble and shaming his parents and grandfather? Moreover, even though we might attribute Richard's sitting alone to a developmental snag, we are not aware of what that snag is. Is it shyness? Is it a lack of self-confidence? Either one could account for the knife episode. What better way to make contact with other students or to overcome a feeling of inadequacy than to commit an act of great risk? If Richard had one of these possibilities as a motive, did he have it consciously or subconsciously? If he had it subconsciously, was he acting freely?

Purpose and Judgment

The Richard Dobbins case also entails purpose, judgment, decision, and deliberation. What is the aim of the appeals hearing? What is the point of the weapons policy? What is the objective of the alternative school? What, if anything, was Richard trying to accomplish through his misdeed? While a judgment of the worth of the hearing's purpose is not at issue in the case, a judgment of the value of an opportunity for appeal was at least implicitly on the mind of Superintendent Delmar and his assistant when they originally discussed the weapons policy and its application. Dr. Cooper defends the worth of the policy's purpose as well as that of the aim of the alternative school. While Mr. and Mrs. Dobbins want to assess whatever goal Richard wanted to accomplish by violating the policy, they do not learn what that goal was. The silence that ensued during the drive home after Richard said that he did not know why he scratched the paint with the knife suggests that his parents regarded him as having no goal at all or as having one he was ashamed to divulge. The silence also intimates that they viewed both options as bad.

Decision and Deliberation

Decision and deliberation lie in the background as well as in the foreground of the Richard Dobbins case. Superintendent Delmar and his advisers presumably deliberated about the best way to bring the weapons situation under control. Even though we can speculate that Richard deliberated whether or not to take his knife to school, we suspect that he did not deliberate the matter very clearly or thoroughly. Also, even though we might suspect that Richard acted impulsively or from a subconscious motive, we have to leave open the possibility that he acted deliberately. Whatever the respective deliberations by Ms. Williams and Dr. Cooper were, they led each to enforce the weapons rule. After receiving Ms. Williams's letter, Richard's parents deliberated about what to do. The hearing can be taken as the major part of a complicated deliberative process, one that came to a close after Dr. Cooper completed her private deliberation over what she had heard at the hearing. Finally, we left Richard's case with his parents pondering whether or not to appeal Dr. Cooper's decision to the board of education.

THE NORMS OF MORAL AGENCY

Moral agents, we have argued, ideally prize knowledge, freedom, purposefulness, and the other features of moral agency. They also have rights and duties relevant to these features. Let us now consider what related standards the participants in the Richard Dobbins case *actually* have. In identifying those standards, we will see that they pose issues that may be resolved by appeal to the norms of moral agency as principles of moral justice.

KNOWLEDGE

The parties appear to esteem knowledge to a notable extent. What has to be known at the hearing is threefold: the specific charges against Richard, the evidence of what Richard did, and the objections by Mr. and Mrs. Dobbins to the charges. Dr. Cooper formally presents the specific charges. Everyone but Richard, who is passive during the hearing, clearly desires to establish the evidence. The objections by Mr. and Mrs. Dobbins articulately emerge during the hearing, and Dr. Cooper records them.

The obvious issue about knowledge at the hearing is the comparative worth of the knowledge sought and the procedures followed in obtaining it. In all cognitive areas, there are recognized methods for acquiring knowledge, and knowledge claims that do not subscribe to those methods are suspect, at least provisionally. In some fields, such as mathematics and science, methods are exact and primary in determining what may count as knowledge. In common sense and other areas, methods are somewhat indefinite and not always primary in determining what may count as knowledge. During the hearing for the Richard Dobbins case, there is a tension between competing methods. The request by Mr. Dobbins for a delay seems to follow the judicial notion that one cannot state objections to a charge until one has had time to study it, whereas the denial by Dr. Cooper follows the administrative principle of efficiency. So there arises this question: Which is the hearing to value more, objections made under conditions of optimal thoughtfulness or objections made under conditions of administrative efficiency? Other methodological conflicts pertain to the gathering of evidence. A student and a teacher are witnesses in the case, but by administrative rule neither is present at the hearing for interrogation. Perhaps they are not present ultimately for reasons of administrative efficiency, but their absence thwarts Mr. Dobbins's legalistic desire to examine all witnesses. That Mr. Jackson found the knife on Richard means it was a fact that Richard violated the weapons policy; but that Mr. Jackson, at least according to Mr. Dobbins, might not have had a legitimate reason to search Richard means that that fact might not count as evidence. Which, then, are more desirable, the facts of the case regardless of how they are known, or the facts of the case as known by certain methodological procedures?

The rights and duties related to knowledge that legally pertain to the participants are set by federal and state laws and by the policies of the school district of Flowers Middle School. At the hearing, Dr. Cooper is the official for interpreting the district policies, but no one there has the authority to assert what rights and duties on knowledge hold under federal or state law. By default, then, the district policies prevail at the hearing. According to the weapons policy, Ms. Williams has the right to recommend the expulsion of Richard, and his parents have the right to appeal that recommendation. Moreover, Dr. Cooper, acting for Superintendent Delmar, has the duty to provide the parents whatever evidence the district has against Richard. In addition, she has the right and duty to determine what evidence will be accepted and how it will be gathered. So, even if Mr. Dobbins happens to be correct in what he dimly regards as Richard's rights under the U.S. Constitution, he cannot operate according to those rights at the hearing. Even if Dr. Cooper happens to have the constitutional duty to present for questioning the teacher and the student who testified against Richard, she does not recognize that duty when directing the meeting.

Freedom

The freedoms valued by the parties of the appeals hearing are freedom of inquiry and personal freedom. Even though all participants approve of freedom of inquiry for the hearing, some prefer one version of this freedom while the others prefer another version. The procedural rules used by Dr. Cooper define the range of freedom approved by the school district. Mr. Dobbins's vague notion of judicial procedure mark the range that he prefers. The former version reflects a preference for administrative efficiency, whereas the latter suggests a special interest in Richard Dobbins's personal welfare. Because the district's procedural rules control the hearing, they determine what rights and duties anyone at the hearing has on freedom of inquiry.

As already suggested, the personal freedom of concern at the hearing is Richard's. No one at the meeting doubts that Richard acted freely on the bus even though only his parents are explicitly interested, albeit only briefly, in his motive for breaking the weapons rule. That Ms. Williams and Dr. Cooper do not explore Richard's motives does not mean that they dismiss motives as insignificant for his action. Indeed, they might regard the investigation of motives as beyond their competence and within the specialty of some psychologist or psychiatrist. But that Mr. and Mrs. Dobbins ask Richard about his motive does not mean that they feel especially competent in getting at the matter. The fact that they only briefly pursue that line of questioning allows that they feel inadequate to the task. That fact also allows other possibilities: The parents do not value his motive very highly, or they are fearful of learning what, if any, motive there is. Because all parties view Richard as violating the weapons rule freely as well as knowingly, they all regard him as liable to some punishment for his deed. Hence, their esteem of personal freedom carries over to those items traditionally associated with freedom coupled with knowledge, namely, responsibility, reward, and punishment.

By school policy and by statute, officials and parents at the hearing have the right to inquire into Richard's motives. That they do not inquire deeply into his motives does not mean that any of them commits a sin of omission. While a right is a freedom of which one *may* take advantage, it is not a freedom of which one always *must* take advantage. In other words, a person may decline to exercise a right, at least, for good reasons. Since neither Ms. Williams, Dr. Cooper, nor Mr. and Mrs. Dobbins exercise the right to consider Richard's motives fully, it does not mean that any of them necessarily has a good reason for not exercising the right. The plea of incompetence does not hold because the officials and the parents could employ a psychologist for interviewing Richard. Adminsitrative efficiency might be a good reason for the officials but not for Mr. and Mrs. Dobbins. The parents' possible fear of finding a dark side to Richard is certainly not a good reason. Also, just not being very interested in motives is patently not a good reason.

Besides asking whether or not school officials or parents have good reasons for not exercising the *right* to explore Richard's motives, we further wonder if any of them has the *duty* to examine his motives. Even though Ms. Williams and Dr. Cooper do not obviously have this duty by school regulations, they might have it perhaps by professional commitment. They are educators, and as such, they might have the obligation to learn about Richard's motives if in so doing they are able to help him educationally. Mr. and Mrs. Dobbins surely have the duty to investigate Richard's motives even though they are not bound by statute to do so. Because they have committed themselves to educating Richard, they are obligated to plumb his motives if, in so doing, they are able to help him with his education.

Purposefulness and Judgment

Purposefulness is generally esteemed at the appeals hearing. The meeting has a goal appreciated by all, namely, a statement of objections by Mr. and Mrs. Dobbins. The weapons policy has a purpose valued by the school officials and presumably by Richard's parents. Mr. Dobbins and Dr. Cooper are especially concerned with the worthiness of the alternative school's purpose. Moreover, Mr. and Mrs. Dobbins are quite interested in the direction of their son's life. However, these people not only esteem some goals and challenge the worth of others but they also appreciate, at least implicitly, the judgmental process by which goals are valued or disvalued. Dr. Cooper apparently approves of the process by which Superintendent Delmar and his assistant determined what the aim of the weapons policy should be. Richard's parents are very careful in assessing alternative options for his life. In addition, they take pains to ensure that their objections to Ms. Williams's recommendation are good ones. The administrative rules controlling the meeting limit the right to judgment by participants. Thus, the rules grant Mrs. Dobbins the right to evaluate the weapons policy as harsh, but they do not give Mr. Dobbins the right to examine certain witnesses so as to judge their credibility. Those rules also assign some duties about judgment. For instance, Dr. Cooper has the duty to assess the objections stated by Mr. and Mrs. Dobbins.

There are several issues relevant to the hearing's norms actually operating on purposefulness and judgment. Even though the purpose of the weapons policy is approved by all parties, is it the highest desirable end? Maybe the policy should aim at the reduction of weapons possession, but perhaps it should aim in addition at something constructive. Because Mr. Dobbins and Dr. Cooper disagree over what is a worthy purpose for the alternative school, they pose the question of what that purpose should be. The serious interest of Richard's parents in their son's well-being in life seems commendable, but it does make us wonder what they specifically have in mind. Do they mean material prosperity, career success, a feeling of contentment, or something else? If any of these, is it the most desirable end that Richard might pursue? Finally, the assignment of rights and duties on judgment by Dr. Cooper's administrative rules raises the question of whether or not people involved in the hearing have such rights and duties that originate some place else, namely, moral agency. Do Ms. Williams and Dr. Cooper have judgmental rights and duties that derive from their being moral agents with a professional interest in Richard's education? Do Mr. and Mrs. Dobbins have such rights and duties that derive from their being moral agents with a parental interest in Richard's education?

Decision and Deliberation

Given Ms. Williams's leadership position at Flowers Middle School, we presume that she appreciates decision making and the deliberation that accompanies it. But given her relief after learning of the reduced punishment for Richard, we also suspect that she would have preferred being able to decide upon a recommendation other than the one she made. She appears, then, to have been caught between administrative rules and her own thinking of what should be done. The former gave her no right to do other than she did; indeed, those rules made it her duty to do what she did. Yet, if she had strong reasons for deciding upon a different course of action, what should she have done?

By contrast, the Dobbinses were in a more agreeable position. While they plainly disapprove of Ms. Williams's recommendation, they have the right under the given administrative rules to file objections against it. They also have the right under those rules to appeal Dr. Cooper's decision even though they are not sure that they should exercise that right. While they disapprove of Richard having to attend the alternative school for even half a semester, they weigh that negative factor against other prudential considerations, such as the stress and distraction to which another appeal might subject Richard. But do the Dobbinses have a duty dictated by something other than law or prudence to appeal Dr. Cooper's decision? What might the source of that duty be?

Apparently, Dr. Cooper values the appeals hearing as a way of helping her to deliberate what to decide about Richard's case. She also appears to find administrative decision making and deliberation worthy matters. Yet, the fact that she decides upon a punishment for Richard that is different from the one specified in the weapons policy leaves us wondering if her decision rests upon administrative reasons alone. By what official rule does she reduce the punishment? If the rule is unofficial, how binding is it in an administrative procedure? Perhaps Dr. Cooper is relying upon nonadministrative reasons, such as common sense and professional standards. If so, does she have the authority to decide upon the basis of such reasons? Also, if Dr. Cooper finds it right to depart from the wording of the weapons policy, should she urge Superintendent Delmar to consider amending that policy?

CRITICISM OF THE VIEWS OF JUSTICE

The appeals hearing on the Richard Dobbins's case, we have explained, is concerned mainly with justice. Much of the discussion focuses on the question of what is a fair punishment for Richard, and another sizable portion dwells on the issue of what are fair procedures for gathering evidence against Richard and for directing the appeals hearing. Answers to these questions, we also have noted, may come from the standpoint of legal justice, which may be judicial or administrative, or the standpoint of moral justice. At the appeals hearing, the operating standpoint is administrative. Strictly from that standpoint, a fair punishment for Richard is what the weapons policy dictates, and a fair way to gather evidence against Richard and to regulate the hearing is whatever the rules of the school district allow. To be sure, administrative regulations can lead to full legal justice only if they are consistent with constitutional and statutory laws. But whether or not any of the administrative rules governing Richard's case violate constitutional or statutory law is unsettled. We do not, however, have to resolve this matter in order to address the questions of justice embedded in the hearing, for we will approach them from the standpoint of moral justice, which rests on the norms of moral agency. Being superior to any other kind of justice, moral justice can be used as a vantage point by which to assess claims of justice from either an administrative or a judicial standpoint.

Was Dr. Cooper fair in not granting Richard's parents a delay so that they could study the formal charge thoroughly? It is arguable that she was not even administratively fair. After all, the purpose of the appeals hearing was to hear the parents' objections to the charge against

Richard. What, then, is the sense of hearing objections that are not based upon full knowledge of what the charge is? Dr. Cooper, nevertheless, does have a plausible defense: The formal charge adds little that was not already said in the letter from Ms. Williams. So, if it is true that the two statements of the charge are substantially the same, there cannot be an objection to Dr. Cooper's action from the viewpoint of moral agency. A delay would not enable the Dobbinses to be better informed about the charge than they already are. Apparently, the two statements are materially equivalent.

But Dr. Cooper's decision not to provide Richard's parents with the opportunity to interrogate the student and the teacher seems much less defensible. The charge against Richard was based largely upon what the student saw and what the teacher heard from the student, but only Ms. Williams interviewed these two witnesses. Nobody, it appears, double checked the student's report. According to the norms of moral agency, action should be grounded upon full knowledge. A full knowledge of the Richard Dobbins's case would include a thorough questioning of the student and the teacher. Dr. Cooper's decision, however, presumes that full knowledge is not important or that Ms. Williams's account of the veracity of the reports by the student and the teacher is complete and reliable. Giving the parents the opportunity to interview these witnesses would have provided some inconvenience for them, but their testimony in the case was extremely serious for Richard.

Dr. Cooper's decision not to permit interrogation of the student and the teacher led Mr. Dobbins to object to the search of Richard and the discovery of the knife in his possession. Nevertheless, the moral unfairness of that decision does not mean that including Richard's possession of the knife as evidence in the case is unjust too. Even though the absence of interrogation of the student and the teacher makes the justice in the search and discovery problematic, it does nothing about the fact that Richard had a knife on the bus. He admitted that much to his parents. Moreover, there is no firm reason to believe that Mr. Jackson's search showed disrespect toward Richard as a moral being. Under the circumstances, Mr. Jackson should have searched Richard. His job as a security officer gave him a special responsibility to look for weapons. He supposedly had no reason to doubt the word of the teacher. Finally, Mr. Jackson's search of Richard did not morally harm him. It did not involve, for instance, threat or torture.

With respect to freedom of inquiry in the case, there is a definite difficulty. By the rules governing the investigation of Richard, Ms.

Williams had the freedom to interrogate the student and the teacher, but by the rules governing the appeals hearing, Mr. and Mrs. Dobbins did not have this freedom. This situation is morally unfair. According to the norm of moral rights, moral agents must respect the rights of one another. If Ms. Williams has the right to query the student and the teacher, then the Dobbinses also have that right, for they have the same interest in these witnesses that Ms. Williams has in them. Hence, Dr. Cooper morally should have respected the right of the Dobbinses to question these witnesses. In arranging a meeting for the questioning, she certainly could have scheduled it for after-school hours or at some other time to minimize inconvenience for all concerned.

There also is a difficulty related to Richard's personal freedom. No responsible party seriously probed Richard's motives for carrying the knife to school and using it on the bus. This neglect does not necessarily mean that anybody disrespects Richard's motives, but because the neglect keeps both school officials and parents from understanding Richard's motives, it does mean that they will not be able to assess the degree of responsibility that Richard had in breaking the weapons rule. If Richard had motives over which he exercised control, then he is much more responsible than if he had coercive or subconscious ones. Greater responsibility should bring greater punishment. Hence, it is unjust to assign Richard a punishment without taking into account the extent of his responsibility determined by his motives.

The purpose of the school district's weapons policy is to reduce the possession of weapons by students. More specifically, the expulsion of those with weapons and enrollment of them in the alternative school for two semesters is to reduce weapons possession. At first glance, this purpose is in line with a traditional view of the function of punishment. As usually understood, punishment involves the imposition of something unpleasant upon a person for breaking a rule. This imposition is traditionally seen as having one or more of several functions. It is simply retributive; that is, it serves merely as a payback for the violation of a rule. It is also reformative; that is, it is a means for reforming the culprit. Or it is preventive; that is, it is a way for deterring future violations by other persons as well as by the culprit. Being conceived to reduce the possession of weapons, the punishment embodied in the weapons policy has a preventive function. On second glance, however, this stated punishment might not be an actual punishment for some violators of the weapons policy; it might not impose anything unpleasant for them. There is no doubt that attending the alternative school will be painful for Richard, but it is doubtful that attending that school will be any more disagreeable to some other students than their attending a regular school. In actuality, then, Richard will be punished while others probably will not be. It follows that the weapons policy is unfair in the punishment that it assigns in blanket fashion.

Of course, that a policy intends to be preventive does not mean that it has to be punitive. Violations can be prevented without deliberately punishing anybody. Culprits can be incarcerated in "country club" prisons. Also, they can be concentrated in an institution for behavioral control that is free of any infliction of pain. The alternative school that Richard is to attend resembles such an institution. By Dr. Cooper's own statement, deterrence is achieved by placing violators of the weapons policy in the alternative school for control purposes. She never claims that enrollment in the school is to be punitive. We, then, are confused in criticizing the policy for having an inappropriate punishment clause. But even if the policy seeks behavioral control without punishment, it suffers a problem of fairness. The policy aims to control the behavior of students, regardless of their differences, in a uniform way. Each and every guilty student is to be enrolled in the alternative school for a period equivalent to two semesters even if a student can learn to modify his or her behavior under some lesser measure. It simply is not fair for the policy to subject all guilty students to the same treatment when some of them might not need it or might even deserve a different treatment for the policy's purpose.

Superintendent Delmar might object, however, that we have overlooked a key point about the weapons policy. While it sends culprits to the alternative school primarily to facilitate the control of their behavior, it also sends them there secondarily to send a warning to all other students. But to whom is enrollment in the alternative school an effective warning? Certainly not to the students who see nothing unpleasant about the alternative school. Certainly not to Richard, who violated the policy regardless of any stigma attached to the alternative school. Perhaps the policy sends an effective warning to only those students who are interested in carrying weapons but at the same time perceive the alternative school as an undesirable place to be.

The alternative school certainly is not a concentration camp, but it is a school whose avowed primary purpose is to concentrate troublesome students for more effective control. Even though this purpose might be morally defensible, it is, nevertheless, symptomatic of injustice in the school district's distribution of goods and services for the moral growth of its students. In other words, it suggests that distributive justice in its moral sense is at least peripherally related to the Richard Dobbins's case.

That kind of justice is of some concern for Richard, in particular. While he seemingly can have access, by virtue of his parents' wealth, to all the goods and services he needs for his moral development, he does not have access to psychological counseling, which he seemingly needs. Perhaps his parents have not made such counseling available to him because of some oversight on their part, but maybe they have withheld that service because they cannot face the fact that he might have a psychological weakness. If the former is the explanation, then they are guilty of thoughtlessness requiring correction, or compensatory justice, but they are not guilty of distributive injustice. If, however, the latter is the explanation, they are not treating their son fairly in a distributive way, for they want to protect their feelings, which they should be able to deal with, at the expense of his moral health.

Moreover, distributive justice is probably relevant to many other students in the school district. Despite the alternative school's behavioral controls and its certified education program, the institution does not meet the moral needs of many of its students, who, according to both Mr. Dobbins and Dr. Cooper, eventually end up in penal institutions. It might be that even with a radically reformed curriculum the school might not help these students, for it might be that by the time they reach the alternative school they are already beyond its help. Thus, we wonder if Superintendent Delmar, the school board, and other leaders of the school district's community have developed any non-alternative-school programs for "at risk" students. If these leaders have developed such programs and have duly found that such programs, regardless of variety and revision, are not effective, then they have done all that justice requires of them. But if they have not developed such programs and duly revised or replaced them, they have committed a breach of distributive justice in that they have not attempted to provide all students with goods and services needed for their moral development.

While judgmental processes by which purposes were chosen for the weapons policy, the alternative school, and Richard Dobbins were thoughtful, they suffered weaknesses that underlay the problems of justice connected with Richard's case. We have associated a major problem of the weapons policy with its punitive element: The stated punishment for violators seems inappropriate, for different reasons, to

Richard and to many "at risk" students. We suspect that the judgmental process in which Superintendent Delmar, his assistant, and the school board engaged to determine the policy's punishment factor lacked adequate questioning. More specifically, we suspect that neither the superintendent, his assistant, nor the board asked if violent students were the only ones who might carry weapons to school or why punishment should be uniform for all violators. Indeed, we wonder if they considered that punishment might be reformative as well as preventive or retributive. If they had asked these questions, they well might have concluded that the policy's punishment should be especially reformative for those students susceptible to moral improvement.

It is likely that similar questions were not asked about the purpose of the alternative school. To describe that institution as an alternative school is to suggest that it is an institution aiming to provide an educational program that is adapted to students who have failed to benefit educationally from standard schools. Ostensibly, then, the alternative school supposedly has a special educational mission. In reality, however, it has the mission of a warehouse. It functions as a place mainly to store and control, not educate, students with serious conduct problems in the standard schools. Even if we allow that the school district has students who can be controlled only in such a warehousing institution, we strongly doubt that all students who have committed serious breaches of behavior should be in such an institution. We suspect that some could benefit from a special program designed primarily for improvement through moral, as well as purely academic, education.

Perhaps the main difficulty with the judgmental processes in which Superintendent Delmar, his assistant, and the school board engaged was not that they by themselves did not think of these questions. Rather, the difficulty might have been that they did not invite others to participate in the processes who might have helped to formulate the questions. Dr. Cooper, as well as Ms. Williams and other principals, might have helped. Reflective parents and social agency representatives also might have helped. Too many cooks spoil the soup, to be sure; but suggestions often help the chef to improve the soup.

There is a similar unfortunate isolation in the judgmental processes undertaken by Richard's parents. The viewpoint from which they typically approach Richard's case is that of prudence. That is, they usually consider it in the light of what is best for their son. Yet, we suspect that another viewpoint, an unspoken one, might be involved too. By failing to ponder Richard's behavior of sitting apart from the other students in his classes or to probe his motivations for carrying the knife to school, the parents suggest that they do not want to learn undeniably that their son might suffer a psychological problem; thus, they are thinking more of themselves than they are of Richard. Hence, it is possible that they basically are operating from an egotistical, or self-centered, viewpoint, which means that their conscious concern with his welfare is a result of a subconscious selfish concern with their own welfare. If the Dobbinses were less defensive in talking about Richard with his teachers, Ms. Williams, and Dr. Cooper, they might find their prudential and possibly egotistical viewpoints challenged by a moral viewpoint. Also, if they consulted with a family psychologist, they might be able to come to grips with any weaknesses underlying Richard's behavior and with whatever needs to be done to help him. Interactions of these kinds, however, usually take place only when schools are structured to facilitate them, not only by encouraging teachers, adminsitrators, and parents to discuss serious conduct problems together but also by guiding parents toward psychological counseling when it seems needed. In addition, family psychologists must be prepared to work with schools rather than apart from them as they frequently do.

The deliberations leading to the decisions on what to do about Richard undoubtedly are earnest and principled; nevertheless, they contain difficulties. The first deliberation is undertaken by Ms. Williams to decide whether or not to recommend that Richard be disciplined. As far as it goes, the deliberation might be faultless. The problem is that it is necessarily quite restricted, for it can entertain only two alternatives. One is to recommend Richard for disciplining and thus for enrollment in the alternative school for two semesters; the other is to cover up the fact that Richard had violated the weapons policy. Even though Ms. Williams sees no good reason for placing Richard in the alternative school for two semesters, she also sees no good reason for covering up his misdeed. Whichever option she takes, then, she takes one that she does not find defensible. Her only reason for recommending discipline for Richard is that as a principal she has a duty to uphold the weapons policy. The unfortunate thing, of course, is that the weapons policy could have been constructed with a greater range of punitive options, some of which Ms. Williams might find especially appropriate for Richard.

Dr. Cooper also faces the problem of restricted options in her deliberations. The weapons policy apparently gives her only two alternatives: Accept Ms. Williams's recommendation and enroll Richard in the alternative school for two semesters, or reject Ms. Williams's recommendation as not sufficiently substantiated. Because she does not reject the recommendation, she then presumably must send Richard to the alternative school for the mandated period. But she does not. Like Ms. Williams, Dr. Cooper presumably regards the punishment dictated by the weapons policy as inappropriate, but unlike Ms. Williams, she does not exactly follow the policy. What other option then does she consider in her deliberation? Perhaps she is fed up with Superintendent Delmar's rigidity and is considering what is the educationally defensible thing to do. But perhaps she has private permission from Superintendent Delmar to use her own discretion in cases where punishment by the policy is plainly excessive. We hope that she has the second option, for it means that the superintendent is not really as thoughtless as the case initially suggests. Nevertheless, even this option is problematic, for to the public, it makes Dr. Cooper appear to be undercutting both the policy and Ms. Williams, thereby undermining parental and student respect for the policy and Ms. Williams.

Finally, the deliberation by the Dobbinses as to whether or not to appeal Dr. Cooper's decision to enroll their son in the alternative school for part of a semester is troublesome from the standpoint of moral agency. In one respect, the deliberation is estimable, for it takes into account the harm that additional stress by another appeal might bring to Richard. This recognition by the Dobbinses, however, is from a prudential, not a moral viewpoint. It is principally a consideration merely of whether or not additional stress will interfere with Richard's progress toward a successful life; it does not include the possibility that the stress might interfere with his moral development. Moreover, this recognition subordinates the question of the moral justice of Dr. Cooper's decision to Richard's welfare. In other words, the Dobbinses do not ask if it is defensible to play down moral justice in favor of their son's welfare. They do not even ask if there is some way to pursue the moral justice issue without placing more stress upon Richard.

CONCLUSIONS

Having raised questions of moral justice in the case of Richard Dobbins, we will now suggest answers to those questions. While the proposed answers address Richard's case especially, they also relate to similar cases.

1. The accused should have at a reasonable point prior to a hearing a full statement of charges. Without an advance complete statement of charges, the accused cannot adequately prepare responses. In Richard's case, the discrepancies between Ms. Williams's statement of charges and that read by Dr. Cooper are immaterial, but they might have been substantial. Requiring a full pre-hearing statement of charges reduces the likelihood of significant differences. Dr. Cooper could have sent a copy of the formal charges in sufficient time to the Dobbinses simply by delaying the hearing for a few days.

2. The freedom to search for evidence must be the same for both parties. Otherwise, the right to seek knowledge for making a moral judgment is not equally respected. Mr. and Mrs. Dobbins, then, should have been allowed to question both the student and the teacher who brought their son under suspicion.

3. In searching for evidence, a party, whether accuser or accused, may examine another moral agent only if that party has good reasons for investigating the latter agent and only if that party uses procedures that are defensible. Otherwise, the searcher neither acts rationally nor respects the moral agency of the latter. Apparently, Mr. Jackson had a good reason to search Richard and employed reasonable measures in the search.

4. All known evidence in a moral case must be admissible for consideration. This rule holds even if the evidence is the product of an improper inquiry. That the evidence appears because of an illicit search means that the investigator is morally blameworthy but not that the evidence should be excluded. Moral judgments are rational; they rest upon all known evidence. Hence, there is a contradiction in excluding from consideration known facts of a case. Of course, if the irregularity of an investigation puts into doubt the authenticity of some alleged evidence, it is grounds for excluding that so-called evidence until its authenticity is established, if ever. Hence, even if Mr. Jackson had searched Richard without sufficient reason, his discovery of the knife would have been admissible as evidence. It was corroborated by the teacher's testimony and by Richard's confession.

5. Punitive sanctions in codes of behavior must allow for a weighing of the motives, circumstances, and past behavior of agents. It follows that they also must provide an array of punishment guidelines related to the material differences among culprits. The weapons policy oper-

ating in the case of Richard Dobbins does not allow for an assessment of these factors, and the hearing does not make a serious effort to weigh them. Moreover, the policy does not contain different punishments related to differences among its violators. If the policy had allowed differential punishment, it would have enabled Ms. Williams to make a more reasonable recommendation than the one she had to make, and it would have saved Dr. Cooper from making a discretionary decision with unfortunate outcomes.

6. The punitive sanction of a student conduct policy must support the sanction's purpose. If the specified punishment supposedly aims at deterrence or reform, it must be such that it is likely to lead to that end. The punishment mandated by the weapons policy in Richard's case does not seem especially relevant to its avowed aim of deterrence.

7. Judgments and deliberations about student conduct must be from a moral viewpoint. When they have to take administrative or prudential concerns into account, they should couch them within the framework of moral agency. Administrative rules must be morally acceptable, and a person's welfare must be consistent with moral values, rights, and duties. Thus, Dr. Cooper needs to temper her penchant for administrative efficiency with moral principle, and Mr. and Mrs. Dobbins need to articulate their son's welfare within the framework of moral agency.

8. Regulations for student discipline must be supplementary to the moral education of students. That is, they are to promote the development of students as moral agents either by the deterrence of its disruption or by the moral reform of errant students. While the weapons policy in the case of Richard Dobbins succeeds in deterring some disruptive behavior, it appears to do little or nothing for the moral development of its violators.

9. Schools must have programs and services that relate to the special moral development needs that students have. For instance, there should be moral education programs for "at risk" students and consultation with parents on probable psychological difficulties of their children. If Superintendent Delmar had instituted such programs and services for his district, he probably would not have eliminated all serious conduct problems, but he and his schools might have helped some students, including Richard Dobbins, from having such problems.

10. Those who make regulations for student discipline should seek optimal input for their deliberations and judgments. With such input, they will have an enhanced opportunity to be aware of the impact of proposed rules on the moral values, rights, and duties of students; on

the connections of proposed rules with the moral education of students; on logical discrepancies between the intentions of punitive sanctions and what the sanctions are; and on the likely effectiveness of proposed regulations. Superintendent Delmar, it will be remembered, consulted with only his assistant and the school board when formulating the weapons policy.

_____ 5 _____

Teacher Evaluation

In recent decades, there has been much criticism of instruction in public schools. Some commentators have charged that the teachers in those schools must be held accountable for the reported national decline in student learning. Others have held that alternative routes to traditional teacher certification should be used, that proven instructional practices must be employed, that tenure must be abolished, and that deadwood must be removed. Still others have maintained that instructors should be paid primarily according to merit. A few have proposed that in the long run higher salaries and increased social respect for teachers will attract more people to the field who have greater talent.

Regardless of the diversity in their remedies, the critics seem unanimously agreed that public school teaching can improve only if it undergoes regular evaluation. Periodic instructional assessment is necessary for us to tell which teachers are responsible for drops in learning, which alternative certification routes are worthwhile, which teachers are effective, which ones should be released, and which ones deserve higher salaries. This broad support has led many school districts to adopt measures for the evaluation of instruction. The responsibility for applying these measures has fallen mainly to principals and assistant principals. Carrying out this responsibility has created some tension between teachers and administrators. This tension usually has taken the form of anxiety in teachers, but it occasionally has expressed itself through strong complaints by teachers receiving negative evaluations.

INSTRUCTIONAL EVALUATION AT PULASKI ELEMENTARY

For a long time, Rachel Hopper has been a strong believer in instructional assessment. During her years as a teacher and as an assistant principal, she became convinced that the large majority of teachers are competent and industrious but that some should not be in the schools. The latter, she concluded, retain their positions because they cooperate with administrators, they have friends in high places, or they have negligent supervisors. She eventually resolved that if she ever became a principal, she would put into operation an effective program of teacher evaluation. Meanwhile, she would do whatever she could, as an assistant principal, to help classroom teachers with instructional problems. Ms. Hopper received the desired opportunity when she became the principal of Pulaski Elementary School, which was in a neighboring district.

Two years before Ms. Hopper took the principalship, the school board of the Lincoln School District, where Pulaski is located, gave its newly appointed superintendent a mandate to improve the quality of instruction in the district's schools. The new superintendent recognized that not only his career advancement but his job security depended on the successful execution of his charge. Even though he was not profoundly informed about instructional improvement, he did have some stock ideas on how to attain it. He soon began replacing incumbent principals with personnel whom he thought would be especially talented for and dedicated to instructional improvement. Upon appointing Ms. Hopper to Pulaski, he reminded her, as he reminded all other new principals, of his determination to improve teaching in the district. He explained that he soon would issue district standards to guide the assessment of faculty for tenure and for merit pay. He also mentioned to Ms. Hopper that she would be permitted to nominate a person to assist her in carrying out this evaluation program at her school and in doing whatever else she thought would help improve instruction there. While Ms. Hopper believed that evaluation for retention and salary decisions might conflict with efforts to solve problems in classroom instruction, she thought that she could keep the two from interfering with each other, especially if she could have Richard Lopez for her assistant principal.

Shortly after her appointment, Ms. Hopper nominated Mr. Lopez as her assistant. She had known him as a kindred spirit in the district where she had previously worked. He, too, was an assistant principal there who was especially interested in instructional supervision, but he, too, had to spend more time with bus schedules and discipline problems than with helping teachers. He saw working with Ms. Hopper as a notable professional opportunity, and he readily accepted the offer to be her assistant.

Two months before the start of school, the two of them began working on a program for the improvement of teaching in Pulaski Elementary. Ms. Hopper explained that she wanted to supplement the superintendent's assessment guidelines for retention and salary with a way to identify and correct problems in classroom instruction at the school. While evaluation is necessary for salary and retention decisions, it also is needed for helping teachers to become better in the classroom. The important thing, she added, is not to let the former interfere with the latter. Ms. Hopper further stated that Mr. Lopez would have the responsibilty of working with the teachers on their instructional problems and that she would look after the evaluations for retention and salary decisions. While she allowed that Mr. Lopez should keep her informed of progress in instructional improvement overall for the school, she emphasized that his task was to help teachers, not to be a secret conduit of information on their strengths and weaknesses. Mr. Lopez readily agreed.

A week before the school year began, there was a meeting of the Pulaski faculty with the superintendent, who formally introduced Ms. Hopper and Mr. Lopez and summarized his guidelines for the evaluation of instructors. Each faculty member annually would undergo in the fall an announced observation while conducting a class in a basic subject, and each annually would undergo in the spring an unannounced observation while conducting a class in a different basic subject. Retention and salary decisions would be communicated late in the school year.

While listening to the superintendent, Rachel Hopper realized that he had not informed her whether or not he wanted to see copies of her evaluations. Several days later she learned from the associate superintendent that she was to keep the copies on file until they were requested by the superintedent. After the departure of the superintendent from the faculty meeting, Ms. Hopper explained Mr. Lopez's special role as instructional supervisor, mentioning his professional experience and keen interest in that role.

Then Mr. Lopez explained how he meant to operate. While he would be talking with teachers in the hallways and in their classrooms, he would not be seeking gossip from them about one another. He also mentioned that he would not be looking over their shoulders or questioning students and parents behind their backs. All teaching, he continued, has difficulties. Some problems, however, are bigger than others and what is a large problem for one teacher is not one for another. So, he stressed that he wanted each teacher to feel free to tell him about instructional experiences that the teacher viewed as especially difficult. He would do all that he could to help each teacher overcome what each perceived to be major obstacles to his or her teaching. So, Richard summarized, his job would not be to rank Pulaski's teachers; rather, it would be to help them with those instructional matters they regarded as especially troublesome.

THE CASE OF MARGARET FEISTER

On a Monday afternoon in late spring, Margaret Feister waited in the reception area of the principal's office in order to see Ms. Hopper, who was finishing a parental conference. During her eight years at Pulaski, Ms. Feister has gained a reputation among her colleagues as a dedicated and above-average teacher. She has been known to be absent only for serious reasons. More importantly, she has a reputation for being prepared for her classes, for trying new ways of teaching, and for taking pains to ensure that the large majority of her students were ready for the next grade. However, Ms. Feister has also acquired the reputation of being a professional loner. Even though she has been friendly with other teachers, she has not talked with them much about her teaching. When she does talk with them about it, she only makes brief and glib comments. Moreover, she has never been very active on faculty committees for instructional improvement. What other instructors have known about her teaching has come mainly from inference.

It bothered Ms. Feister that she now might have to discuss her instruction with Ms. Hopper. The previous Friday, the Pulaski teachers received notice of their salaries for the coming year. Ms. Feister's salary increase was 3.5 percent, which, according to newspaper accounts over the weekend, was average for the district. This was the first time that she had not gotten an above-average raise. At first she began to wonder what she might have done wrong in her teaching; she next started to think that Ms. Hopper might have made a mistake in assessing her instruction. Only by talking with Ms. Hopper could she learn the reason for her disappointing raise. Early Monday morning she requested and got an appointment with Ms. Hopper for that afternoon.

After Ms. Hopper finished conferring with the parent, she invited Ms. Feister into her office, where the two of them sat in modest but comfortable chairs facing each other. "Margaret," the principal said after some opening pleasantries, "how may I help you this afternoon? Is the Wilson boy getting under your skin?"

"No, the problem is not a student. I am afraid it's my salary or my teaching. The raise you gave me, I believe, is average, which means, I suppose, that my teaching has been average this year. While I realize that average is nothing to be ashamed of, I expect more of myself. Could you please tell me what you saw wrong in my performance when you did the evaluations?"

When Ms. Hopper prepared the memos on salary raises, she concluded each of them with the courtesy, "If you have questions about this matter, feel free to see me about them." She expected a few complaints, but she was not prepared for the uncertainty she was experiencing now that someone had accepted the invitation. During the year, she had evaluated thirty teachers twice each, and she could not remember all the particulars of each observation. Indeed, she was having difficulty in recalling more than a few details from either of her observations of Margaret. She had taken notes, but they were in a file drawer, not before her. She instinctively stalled by describing the evaluation process she followed in determining that Margaret's performance, regardless of its specific strengths and weaknesses, ranked in the middle tier, which included most of the school's teachers.

Ms. Feister feigned attentive listening, barely hiding her rising impatience. Surely, she thought, Rachel Hopper must know that I am aware of the evaluation process; she has explained it to the faculty three times this year. Does she take me for a dunce, or did she not comprehend my question? I'll try again. "Ms. Hopper, I have no questions about the process you followed. The guidelines strike me as sensible; they certainly are a lot more relevant than the ones we had under the previous superintendent. What is bothering me is that I simply do not know where my teaching has gone wrong this year. Would you please tell me exactly why you judged it to be no more than average?"

At this point, Ms. Hopper began to recall some details about Margaret's instruction. "I would not say that your teaching has gone wrong this year, but I do think there are a few places where it can be strengthened. After I visited your room in the fall, you might remember, I mentioned some things to you that I liked very much about your instruction. You were very familiar with the lesson material; you were enthusiastic; and you had control of the students. I also said that there were a few things that you should be aware of. One of the objectives on your lesson plan was not specific enough to tell what would count as its achievement. There were one or two things you were having the students do that I could not link to the learning activities on your lesson plan. In addition, there were two children not participating in the class. They were quiet, but they were not involved."

"Yes," said Margaret, "I remember our conversation. I thought it was good of you to take the time for a thorough review with each of the staff. But, as I explained then, I do not know that each and every objective of every day has to be as specific as you seem to want. I realize that the district guidelines want the objectives to be specific, but I cannot believe the superintendent intends that every single objective must be precisely measurable. Sometimes I use loose objectives for guides toward something more specific. Also, I do not know that everything I have my students do can be directly connected with preconceived learning activities. After all, teaching should allow for some spontaneity and creativity by students as well as instructors. Moreover, as I mentioned last fall, the two students not engaged in the class are very slow learners. They have been at least two grades behind for the past three years; they have been socially passed. There is no way that I can work with them and get the other twenty-seven students ready for the sixth grade."

Ms. Hopper felt Margaret's present reply more strongly than she had heard the one in the fall. At that time the response had been somewhat quiet, tentative, and reluctant; it did not have the energy, confidence, and forthrightness of the present one. Nevertheless, Ms. Hopper resumed her explanation after only a momentary pause. "Without naming names, Margaret, I have to say that other teachers had all their objectives in order and had all their students involved. Also, I have to mention that during this spring's observation of your class, one of your written objectives was on the general side, that very few learning activities were listed, and that the same two students were not participating. One thing I looked for in the second observation was improvement over the fall, and I did not see it in those respects. But I want to emphasize, Margaret, that everything else I saw of your teaching was very good."

"Thanks, Ms. Hopper; it is kind of you to say that. Nevertheless, I want to explain something. I could have written down something on the lesson plan to make it look as though I had nothing but measurable objectives, and I could have restricted the students to stated learning activities. Also, I could have talked occasionally to those two students. But I am not like that. I take my teaching too seriously to pretend that I am following guidelines to the letter. I have been getting good results with the large part of my students for over five years, and there are very few teachers here who can say that. Once again, I am not objecting to the district guidelines or to your criticism of my instruction. On the other hand, maybe there is something about the guidelines that I do not like. I guess what I do not like is that my instruction is rated by these observations and not by its effectiveness. Should not that be a standard of instructional quality?"

"Actually, Margaret, the superintendent wants us to consider effectiveness. After all, it does not matter much if a teacher performs very well during the observations but has students who do not do well. So, let me see if I can explain how I have related my observations of your teaching to its effectiveness. I am aware of your success in getting the great majority of your students ready for the work in their next grade. But during both of my visits to your class I was concerned by the two students who were not included in the class work that was underway. To be frank, I had to wonder if they were being prepared for next year. As I have mentioned already, other teachers at the school include their slow students in their regular classes in some way. So, when I measured your effectiveness, I had to weigh it against the success of those instructors who work with slow students as well as the regular ones. Pardon me, Margaret, but you look puzzled."

"Look, Ms. Hopper, let's be realistic. Those two students were way behind when they came to me last fall, and they will be farther behind when they go to their next teacher. I do not believe that I or any other teacher can help them overcome their handicaps. Maybe other teachers do include their slow students in regular class activities, but I do not know that they have really helped those students catch up in their academic work. If they have, they certainly did not work with the two students in my class." At this point, Margaret Feister noticed that she was talking faster and more intensely than she normally did. She also felt dry and tight in her mouth and throat. It was time to relax a moment.

Ms. Hopper followed Margaret's argument closely, paying special attention to the feeling that increased with it. She, too, thought that a break was in order. "Margaret, I want to continue our discussion by all means; but I need a break before we do. If it is okay with you, I'll get us a couple of colas."

After the break, Margaret Feister resumed the discussion. "Maybe I have failed to mention something. It is true that those two students were not interacting with the rest of the class when you made your observations. But they were not doing just nothing. I do work with these students when I have time to do so. Each time you visited us, they had special assignments to do at their seats while the rest of the class worked with me. I forget what the assignment was the first time, but the second time they were to look at some magazines to find words that they recognized so that they could copy them. I was not free to keep them on task, so they did some idle looking around. But they were not being ignored entirely. Did I tell you any of this last fall?"

"You might have. Unfortunately, I don't remember everything that I should," Ms. Hopper replied. "But my concern is not that those kids were doing nothing; it is that they were not interacting with the others. One thing all students can and need to learn is how to get along with each other. The handicapped have to have greater opportunities to learn this than others require. So, if we simply have them do seat work by themselves, we will not help them improve in their social skills. Even if we cannot increase their academic competence a whole lot, we can build their social skills appreciably. I have seen it happen."

At this point, Ms. Hopper recognized that she had started to lecture. "Look, Margaret, I should not be rattling on like this. You know about the need for socializing students as much as I do. I just want you to know that it's important for you to work more with involving those two students and others like them in the future. They deserve your attention, and I am confident that you can be a great help to them."

"Ms. Hopper, I respect your concern that the handicapped students in this school should receive the educational opportunities appropriate to them. But I want to emphasize that I have not neglected the handicapped in my classes, whether the two of this year or the ones I have had in all my previous classes. I have never had any unusual trouble with the social behavior of such students. What I have a difficulty with is the notion that I must always have them working with other students when they will not have any idea of what the others are doing. All that they will do is be disruptive." Immediately Ms. Feister was aware that she had gone too far, that she had challenged a policy held by a superior. "I am sorry; I should not have said that."

"Margaret, you feel free to say what's on your mind. I can't understand you or the other teachers if I do not know what you're thinking. Besides, I have thick skin. So, let me comment on your last statement. I personally do not believe that you have to include handicapped students in each and every activity in which the others are engaged. But I simply cannot evaluate you positively on your inclusion of handicapped students if you do not have them participating in the class when I am observing it."

"Well, I see your point, Ms. Hopper. You have to evaluate me only by observation, and you make two observations a year. This seems strange, however. I recently figured that a teacher at this school conducts over 900 classes during the school year. That's five classes a day for over 180 days. You have to base your judgment on what happens during only two of those classes. What about the other 900 classes? Are they irrelevant to judging the quality of instruction? Can two observations really tell you about what's happening during the other 900 classes? If they cannot, why bother with them?"

"You have a point, Margaret, and it deserves further consideration. At this time, however, all that I can say is that the evaluation policy we follow comes from the superintendent, and it is not likely to change any time soon. I suspect that it will undergo review eventually, and when it does, I'll see if I can bring your point to the superintendent's attention. Meanwhile, it's the only policy we have. Even if it is not perfect, it is better than the one this district had before."

"Yes, I agree on that; the old one was silly. Anyhow, Ms. Hopper, you have explained matters for me as completely as I should want. Your evaluation and my pay raise both make sense. I have no more questions; if you have none, I'll be on my way."

"I am glad that I was able to make sense of things this time; I don't succeed in doing that very often. Margaret, I am pleased you stopped by; we've gotten to know each other better. By all means, feel free to come by whenever you think I can be of use."

That evening, when Ms. Hopper was reviewing her schedule for the next day, she began to think about her evaluation of Margaret Feister. An undercurrent of puzzlement about it lingered. Why would Margaret have continued with her practice of excluding the two students? She was aware of the importance of the second evaluation, and most other teachers had managed to correct the practices for which they had been faulted. It then occurred to Rachel that Margaret had said nothing during their discussion about changing her way next year. Could it be that she is hopelessly stubborn; could it simply be that she does not know how to conduct a class with handicapped students participating? Maybe Richard Lopez could give her some insight into Margaret's case when they met tomorrow morning for their daily planning session.

Early in the session, Ms. Hopper abruptly asked Mr. Lopez if he had had much contact with Margaret during the year. "Actually," he replied, "I've had some small talk with her almost every day; but I have not spoken with her in depth about anything. Is there something specific you are interested in?"

"Yes, I want to know if she regularly includes all her students in class participation, especially the two handicapped ones. She claims that she usually does, and I have never heard that she does not. But she failed to engage the handicapped students during each of my observations of her. As you know, my evaluations are finished for the year, and anything you can tell me on this will have no bearing on my assessment of her. But it might improve my understanding of her."

"Rachel, I wish I could be of help here, but I doubt that I can. Margaret certainly has not said that she has had a problem with handicapped students in class activities. On the other hand, she has never definitely allowed that she has had any kind of instructional problem. She usually has commented on teaching in general, and the most she has ever said about her own teaching has been that she has continued to enjoy it even though she has not found it any easier. The result is that I've never worked with her on an instructional problem. You may remember that I have had biweekly meetings of the instructional committee this year, and Margaret has served on it. From her comments during meetings of that committee, however, I have gathered no special facts about what goes on in her classroom."

"Well," Ms. Hopper responded, "maybe I need to have the door removed from Margaret's classroom or have a surveillance camera installed in the room. Then I could observe her every day. Seriously, though, Richard, how am I supposed to evaluate someone's instruction for a year by sampling only a tiny fraction of what they are doing? And I'm not talking about just salary in Margaret's case. What's really important there is whether or not she is helping her handicapped students acquire social skills. She says she is, but I do not have direct evidence on the matter."

"I'll keep my ears and eyes open," Mr. Lopez said, "but only in a passive way, you know. Most of the teachers have come to trust me, I think. They have known me for only a few months, but they seem to be more and more comfortable in consulting with me on a number of their problems. So, I don't want to risk undermining the trust that has developed between them and me by being intrusive."

"Richard, I don't want you to upset that trust either," Ms. Hopper said. "But until I learn how Margaret usually deals with her handicapped students, I won't know for sure whether or not any changes need to be made in her teaching. Enough of that for now, however. Let's move on to the next item on today's agenda."

IDENTIFICATION OF THE CENTRAL TOPIC

The central theme of the Margaret Feister case is perhaps not as obvious as that of our previous cases. Actually, several themes quickly come to mind, but under scrutiny they do not, either singly or collectively, provide a comprehensive focus on the case.

One theme is pride. Like Achilles, who stayed in his tent and refused to help his fellow Greek soldiers against the Trojans, Margaret Feister keeps to herself, at least professionally. She does not discuss her teaching specifically with her colleagues or with Mr. Lopez, and she discusses it with Ms. Hopper only reluctantly. She appears to have kept to herself for the reason of pride but not, unlike Achilles, from wounded pride. We sense that she regards herself as so superior to her fellow teachers that she would be demeaning herself by sharing her pedagogical knowledge with people incapable of understanding and appreciating it. Moreover, even though she does not sulk over her raise, she plainly is disturbed by being rated as average. While she is willing to entertain the possibility that her teaching has been faulty, she is quite defensive about Ms. Hopper's criticisms. She never concedes that any of them is valid; she never allows that she will change her ways during the coming year.

But even if we grant that pride is an important theme in the case of Margaret Feister, we are not convinced that it is the central one. It does not seem to require the attention that the case gives to the efforts by Richard Lopez to develop trust in the faculty of Pulaski Elementary School. It does not appear to account for the point that the fairness of the superintendent's policy of two observations a year is questionable. It does not seem to call for all the interplay of feeling during the discussion between Margaret and Ms. Hopper. And it does not appear to make sense of Ms. Hopper's strong concern about knowing how Margaret usually conducts her classroom.

Apart from their problematic connections with Margaret's pride, the qualities of trust, fairness, feelings, and knowledge easily come to mind as candidates for the principal subject matter of her case. They surely receive some emphasis in the case. None of these qualities, however, fares any better than pride does. Each ultimately fails to provide a place for some other of them. But rather than assessing each of them as a theme, we should pause and consider whether or not there is a subject matter in the Margaret Feister case that shows much greater promise of interrelating all the other ones that we have mentioned.

The topic that appears to be central to the case is instructional evaluation. For one thing, instructional evaluation easily allows for the roles played by Richard Lopez and the superintendent as well as that played by Rachel Hopper. Mr. Lopez is interested in instructional evaluation primarily as it affects the improvement of instruction. The superintedent is concerned with it mainly as it shapes tenure and salary decisions. Ms. Hopper is interested in it for both ends. Also, she engages in the tenure-salary type directly and in the improvement type indirectly. For another thing, instructional evaluation allows for the emphasis given to pride, feelings, and knowledge. Instructional evaluation always involves particular persons, and they always have their special character traits. Margaret Feister happens to be proud of herself as a teacher. That pride presents difficulties for the evaluation of her instruction. Moreover, even though the discussion between Margaret Feister and Rachel Hopper aims at a rational explanation and understanding of Ms. Hopper's evaluation of Margaret, it recognizes that these two persons have feelings and that their feelings do relate to the search for explanation and understanding. Finally, Ms. Hopper is seriously concerned with knowing about Margaret's everyday instruction because she is conscientiously responsible for instructional improvement in her school, which presupposes a knowledge of instructional situations there.

THE FEATURES OF MORAL AGENCY

Having settled upon teaching evaluation as the moral topic of the Margaret Feister case, we must recognize that all principles and facts in the case are subject ultimately to understanding and judgment based upon the norms of moral agency. As we have already indicated, moral standards logically are superior to action guides of any other kind, and the facts connected with any moral situation are liable to final judgment based upon moral standards. For moral agents, this means that whatever principles and facts are involved in the evaluation of teaching logically must be compatible with those norms. Consequently, Rachel Hopper's procedures and decisions, Richard Lopez's approach to instructional supervision, Margaret Feister's character, the superintendent's policy on instructional assessment, and all other elements of the case must be compatible with the values, rights, and duties of moral agency. To explain how instructional evaluation in the Margaret Feister case may be understood specifically within the framework of moral agency, we will identify the features of moral agency embedded in the case and then relate the norms of such agency to the case.

Freedom

All parties in Margaret Feister's case act freely. As a condition of his employment, the superintendent was under a directive from his district school board to improve instruction, but he did not have to accept the offered position. More significantly, he was at liberty to formulate and implement his own policy on instructional evaluation.

While Rachel Hopper has to follow the superintendent's policy, she *has to* not in the sense that she is *physically or psychologically compelled to* but in the sense that she is *committed to following the policy as a condition of her employment.* Other indications of her freedom are that she expresses an intention of trying to get changes in the superintendent's policy, that she has input into the selection of her assistant, that she can supplement the superintendent's policy with her own measures for instructional improvement, and that her judgment of Margaret Feister's teaching is not done under duress.

Certainly Richard Lopez acts with liberty. Even though his decision to be Ms. Hopper's assistant puts him in the position of being committed to following her directives as well as those of the superintendent, he has freely decided to be her assistant. Moreover, he has considerable latitude for developing and carrying out his instructional supervision program and has the opportunity to participate in Rachel Hopper's planning sessions.

Margaret Feister, too, acts with liberty. Neither the policies nor the proposals of the superintendent, Rachel Hopper, or Richard Lopez force her to conduct her classes one way or another. Indeed, we get the distinct impression that she runs them as she wants to. She openly discusses her evaluation with Ms. Hopper without any fear of reprisal. When she recognizes that she has directly criticized one of Ms. Hopper's policies, she apologizes not from fear but from her own rule of not pointedly criticizing a supervior's policy.

The only element that seems problematic for Margaret's freedom is her pride. As a character trait, pride is a quality of dispositions, not a special and separate disposition. One is not disposed, for example, to teach and in addition to act proudly. One is inclined, instead, simply to teach with pride. In her teaching, then, Margaret does not have pedagogical habits plus a habit of pride; she has, rather, pedagogical dispositions containing the quality of pride. No distinct habit of pride, then, compels her to teach as she does. Nevertheless, it is possible that the pride qualifying her pedagogical habits might be so powerful as to compel her not only to teach as she does but also to relate to Rachel Hopper, Richard Lopez, and her teaching colleagues as she does. Unfortunately, we do not have a clear idea of how much her pride controls her actions. While we know that Margaret seems to regard her teaching as beyond the competences and appreciation of her colleagues, we cannot infer for that reason that she is subservient to her pride. We could argue that she might have good reasons to look down on her colleagues as teachers. After all, instructional performance supposedly has been a problem at Pulaski Elementary, as well as at other schools in its district. Also, the tenor of the discussion between Margaret and Ms. Hopper suggests that the former would alter her way of teaching if she learned of a defensible reason to do so. So, even though we have to grant that pride colors Margaret's professional character, we cannot conclude that it dominates that character.

Knowledge

Knowledge is another feature of moral agency that is integral to the Margaret Feister case. The superintendent presumably does not have scientific knowledge of how to improve instruction in schools, but he seems convinced that tenure and merit pay will substantially help attain that end. Moreover, he apparently believes that two observations of a teacher per year can provide sufficient information for rating that teacher's performance. It is not clear, however, what the superintendent exactly intends to do with the information that his principals obtain on their teachers. Will he use them as a basis for districtwide staff improvement? Will he use the evaluations as a basis for charting instructional improvement in the district? Will he use them simply as a rationale for telling his school board that any teacher in his district gets tenure or merit pay only if they deserve it? In truth, will he ever look at the evaluations?

In order to encourage her teachers to improve their respective teaching, Rachel Hopper seeks to reward them with tenure and salary increases based upon their individual merit as instructors. To determine that merit, she has to have knowledge of what the teachers do in their classrooms. That knowledge she seeks through two observations of each teacher's classroom performance. That those observations are sufficient to inform her of what a teacher usually does in her classroom is a question during the discussion between Ms. Hopper and Margaret. Yet, as Ms. Hopper intimates by her kidding comment to Richard Lopez about removing the door from Margaret's classroom or installing a surveillance camera in the room, she appears to have no feasible way of obtaining first-hand information about what her teachers regularly do in their classrooms. But the paucity of her direct observations is not the only epistemological difficulty confronting her. After some discussion with Margaret, Ms. Hopper recognizes that what she has observed of the teacher's treatment of the two handicapped students is incomplete. Being contextual, the treatment is knowable only with knowledge of its context. Ms. Hopper's information about that context necessarily comes from Margaret. How reliable is that information, however? Should Ms. Hopper take it at face value, or should she weigh it by its source, namely, a person who conceivably stands to gain by that information as it stands?

Richard Lopez also needs direct knowledge about what goes on in the classrooms of Pulaski Elementary School. Unlike his principal, however, he seeks it not to rate teachers for tenure and salary decisions but to help each of them solve what they individually perceive to be their major instructional problems. While he recognizes that the conditions of teacher perception and voluntariness taint with subjectivity the information that he obtains about instruction in the classrooms, he maintains that the lack of objectivity is a price worth paying in order to gain the trust of teachers and, hence, their openness to talking with him about their instruction. Accordingly, the limitations, which are not principles of epistemological theory, are imposed by Mr. Lopez for practical reasons.

The knowledge relevant to Margaret Feister is mainly pedagogical. She knows what the purpose of her teaching is. She has knowledge of instructional contents, instructional methods, and learning activities. She has information on the backgrounds of her students. In addition, she knows which contents, methods, and activites to select and which organization to give those selected in order to achieve the purposes she has in mind. While she sees herself, perhaps justifiably, as a superior teacher, she is unwilling to share her pedagogical knowledge with colleagues and apparently does not use her colleagues as a source of knowledge about teaching.

In her meeting with Rachel Hopper, Margaret seeks knowledge about her teaching performance. Her interest in this knowledge is mixed. It is partly to learn how to improve her instruction but also partly to revise, perhaps to defend, her estimate of her worth as a teacher. Far from being one-sided, the meeting becomes an interactive examination of Margaret's teaching, Ms. Hopper's expectations, and the superintendent's policy. Through this discussion, Margaret learns some things about her teaching that she probably would not have thought of otherwise. Ms. Hopper, too, learns some things that she probably would not have thought of otherwise. At the end of the discussion, however, Ms. Hopper recognizes that she needs more knowledge about Margaret's teaching, and Margaret leaves no clue as to what impact the information she obtains is likely to have upon her future instruction. Whatever the impact will be, Margaret is not expected to share it with her colleagues any more than she is expected to view them as sources of information for her teaching.

Purpose and Judgment

Another trait of moral agency involved in the Margaret Feister case is purpose. The superintendent explicitly wants to improve instruction in the Lincoln School District; he presumably also has the much broader goal of looking after all the other school problems of the district. On the assumption that the superintendent is prudent, we suspect that he further means to protect his job, which is not covered by tenure.

Rachel Hopper's purposes are extensions of some of the superintendent's. She has the urgent general goal of improving instruction in her school. With respect to this end, she has more specific ones: to award tenure and grant salary increases on the basis of demonstrated desert and to solve classroom instructional problems. Moreover, she apparently seeks to care for the other administrative problems that go along with being an elementary school principal, such as discipline, budgetary needs, building maintenance, and dealing with parental complaints. Being new in the Lincoln district, Ms. Hopper has acquired no tenure there as a teacher, and as a principal, she is not in a tenure-track position. She gives no impression, however, of being preoccupied with job security. Perhaps she assumes that if she does her best as the principal of Pulaski Elementary School, she does not have to worry about retaining her position there.

Richard Lopez's purposes follow from Ms. Hopper's. Overall, his mission is to identify and solve the major classroom instructional problems in Pulaski Elementary School. More specifically, his task is to work with the school's teachers on their self-reported major teaching problems and, in support of that task, to establish a lasting trust with those teachers. Like Ms. Hopper, he does not seem especially concerned with job security.

Some of Margaret Feister's aims pertain to her activities in the classroom. Overall, she wants her students to become ready for their next grade level. The readiness she appears to have in mind allows for social maturity but appears to be mainly academic. Moreover, the readiness is for the class as a whole, not for particular students. A lesser purpose, then, is to provide special learning activities for students who cannot maintain the minimum standards for the class in general. As indicated by her streak of pride, Margaret also seeks to maintain her status as a superior teacher. She apparently does not work at being a good teacher in order to receive superior salary increases, but she does seem to regard her salary increases as public confirmations of her quality as a teacher.

Both the purposes and the actions of moral agents involve judgment. Such agents choose purposes only if they deem them morally worthy, and they decide upon actions for attaining their goals only if, after due deliberation, they judge those actions morally acceptable. Judgment, then, is a characteristic of moral agency that permeates the case of Margaret Feister.

Before the school board of the Lincoln School District hired the superintendent, it had taken the view that instruction in the district's schools needed significant improvement. That the board fully judged the quality of instruction is not at all evident. More specifically, we do not know if the board said that instruction in the schools needed serious improvement because it, on its own or through the services of experts, had gathered information on that instruction and compared it with a definite set of standards for teaching. It simply might have said the schools needed better instruction simply because it believed numerous unsolicited complaints from parents about instruction.

A similar point applies to the superintendent. We know that he was not especially knowledgable about classroom teaching, that he had a charge to improve instruction in the district, and that he hired person-nel and formulated guidelines to that end. What we do not know is if he conducted, personally or through the efforts of experts, an investi-gation of the quality of teaching in the district's schools. In truth, we do not even know if he actually believed that the teaching was seriously deficient. He might have believed only that he needed to do something about improving instruction in the district if he was to keep his job.

With respect to Rachel Hopper, however, the status of judgment is not problematic. She personally rates the instruction of her teachers, including Margaret Feister, using observations and the superinten-dent's guidelines as the basis of her judgments. She deems instructional supervision to be especially important for improving classroom teach-ing. She also, we learned, judges the superintendent's guidelines to need revision. Even though her program for the improvement of instruction in Pulaski Elementary School was not grounded on a preliminary study of that instruction, the program was devised and implemented without a need for such an investigation. The program, whether for faculty ratings or for classroom supervision, does not assume that any or all teachers in the school are deficient, nor does it seek to impose in a blanket fashion a specific approach to instruction. Rather, it allows for the discovery of instructional difficulties, through observation or self-report, only as they relate to individual teachers and further allows for solutions according to the circumstances of the particular situations where the difficulties are identified.

Even though Rachel Hopper has judged Margaret Feister to be an average teacher, she realizes that her assessment rests on seriously incomplete knowledge and a highly questionable procedure. Specifi-cally, she does not know with practical certainty what Margaret's teaching usually is, and because of the superintendent's guidelines, she can observe that teaching for only two sessions each school year. Judgments about practical affairs, however, do not bear logical or scientific certainty. By their nature, such judgments rest on knowledge that is more or less incomplete and follow procedures that are more or less imperfect. We should not be cynical about moral judgments for these reasons, however. Reflecting upon their judgments, agents may gather more knowledge and modify procedures where required and feasible. This is precisely what Rachel Hopper begins to do during the course of her discussion with Margaret Feister and her planning session with Richard Lopez. She comes to recognize that she needs more knowledge about Margaret's teaching and acknowledges that the superintendent's guidelines should be revised. In the future, then, she might modify her judgment of Margaret's instruction.

Because Richard Lopez is committed to instructional supervision, he has judged it to be worthy, and because he regards the trust of teachers to be indispensable for such supervision, he judges it to have a high instrumental value. In trying to help the teachers of Pulaski Elementary School, Mr. Lopez must make judgments. To be sure, he operates on the basis of self-reports from individual teachers, who in effect make judgments about deficiencies in their instruction. Presumably, he will take the self-reports at face value, but he eventually will have to make judgments about what the teachers need to do to overcome their alleged instructional difficulties. Unfortunately, it is not adequately clear how he will proceed. To be sure, he probably will gather information through classroom observations. But what standards of teaching will he follow in determining what a teacher needs to do? Will they be those that the teacher holds? Will they be his own? If the former, what does he do if the teacher cannot articulate what his or her standards are? If the latter, what does he do if a teacher holds standards different from his? Perhaps Mr. Lopez has already considered and answered these questions. If he has not, however, he should become aware of them. He can do this by being attentive to how he goes about making his judgments.

Margaret Feister also makes judgments, about her students, about her teaching, about her colleagues' instruction, about the superintendent's guidelines, and probably about Rachel Hopper's rating of her. Specifically, she has judged that preparing students mainly for next year's academic work is desirable, that her instruction is superior, that her colleagues' teaching is inferior, and that the superintendent's guidelines for classroom observations are inadequate. Even though she makes no explicit assessment of Ms. Hopper's rating of her, she plainly has found fault with it. We should be surprised if, at the end of the discussion with Ms. Hopper, she spoke of the evaluation as satisfactory.

That Margaret has definite pedagogical standards and sticks to them is a mark of integrity on her part. How morally worthy that integrity is depends upon how closely her standards and actions conform to the norms of moral agency.

Decision and Deliberation

Regardless of how thoughtful purposes are, they do not automatically come into existence. They become realized only through actions. Actions may spring from impulse, compulsion, or blind habit; they also may follow from decisions. The actions of moral agents ought to follow from decisions resting on the basis of defensible deliberation, that is, they should be decided upon the weighing of alternative courses of action in view of several factors. The latter are the comparative effectiveness of the various alternatives for attaining the given aims; the facts of the contexts wherein the aims are to be achieved; and the values, rights, and duties of moral agency. In the Margaret Feister case, deliberation is a definite element, but it is clearer in some instances than in others.

The deliberations involved in the decisions of the superintedent are almost entirely unknown to us. While his decisions to replace principals and to base teacher tenure and salary raises on observed instructional performance appear to have in mind the improvement of instruction, they could be more concerned with making a positive impression upon the school board. After all, the superintendent might be more concerned with his job security than with actually improving instruction in the Lincoln School District. Moreover, while these decisions might have taken into account impeccable research on effective ways to improve instruction, they might have followed from nothing more than professional trends or tips from fellow superintendents. In sum, we know what the superitendent's decisions were but not the deliberations underlying them.

Rachel Hopper's deliberations are for deciding upon actions to attain several purposes: to determine tenure and salary increases for the faculty of Pulaski Elementary School, to improve classroom instruction at the school, and to respond to the concerns of Margaret Feister. The facts about the teaching of each faculty member she gathers through classroom observations. The standards she applies to the facts of case are mainly those provided by the superintendent, but they apparently allow some latitude for interpretation. This was suggested by her emphasis upon the desirability of the participation of all students in learning activities. In any event, she uses these facts and standards in deciding whether or not to grant tenure and what salary increase to give.

By what deliberations Ms. Hopper decided that supervision was needed for improvement in classroom instruction we are not aware. Perhaps she was strongly influenced in graduate school courses by professors who advocated instructional supervision. Maybe she had had positive experiences with such supervision earlier in her career. Regardless, because she suspected there likely would be a conflict between her helping teachers improve in classroom performance and her rating them for tenure and salary, she turned over the instructional supervision to Richard Lopez. It is he who has set the self-report criterion for what counts as a major instructional difficulty, who must establish the facts of each reported case, and who must help the instructor in each case to identify and assess the alternatives for overcoming the concerned difficulty. As noted earlier, however, the norms that Mr. Lopez and a given teacher will employ in evaluating alternatives are obscure.

In her interview with Margaret Feister, Rachel Hopper had to make two impromptu decisions affecting the interview's direction. One of those decisions had to be made because of an inadequately formed decision Ms. Hopper had made before the interview. As revealed by her letter informing each teacher of the latter's salary for the next year, Ms. Hopper was willing to examine her rating of any teacher who requested a review. That willingness, however, did not appear to rest upon a definite course of action. Thus, when Ms. Hopper met with Margaret, she felt uncomfortable, for she had not refreshed herself on Margaret's case. Thus, she was not initially conversant with the facts of the case. Upon recognizing her unfamiliarity with these facts, Ms. Hopper could have considered the possibility of pulling Margaret's file and taking a brief time out to refresh herself on the case. We do not know whether or not she entertained this possibility, but we do know that she in effect decided to stall for time while she tried to recollect the details of the case. Luckily she was successful in this effort.

The other impromptu decision was to recommend to Margaret that they take a refreshment break. This decision came at a point in the discussion when Ms. Hopper sensed that Margaret and she both were becoming increasingly tense and emotional. While Ms. Hopper probably did not expect that a discussion with a person about the latter's teaching performance would be free of feeling, she apparently did not think that an emotionally charged interview would be helpful. So, rather than letting the exchange with Margaret get out of control, she decided upon a break as a way of cooling feelings. It proved to be effective.

However, Ms. Hopper's deliberations went beyond her discussion with Margaret. During the evening after the interview, Ms. Hopper wondered how she might obtain more information about Margaret's everyday teaching. Her decision was to raise the issue with Richard Lopez during the next day's planning session. During that session she pursued, briefly, one alternative. She chose to ask what Mr. Lopez could tell of Margaret's teaching without endangering the trust he had earned from Pulaski's instructors. Upon learning that Mr. Lopez knew very little about the matter, Ms. Hopper mentioned the removal of doors and the installation of surveillance equipment as joking expressions of frustration rather than as serious alternatives. When she and Mr. Lopez ceased discussing the Margaret Feister case, she entertained no other definite alternatives, but she leaves the impression that she will continue looking for a suitable way to obtain the information she wants.

Like Ms. Hopper's, Margaret Feister's deliberations were a mix of highly reflective ones and somewhat spontaneous ones. Margaret apparently had carefully decided, with insights gained from her past classroom experience, upon those instructional strategies, curricular contents, and learning activities that would enable her students to achieve the goals she had chosen for them. Moreover, she had brooded during a weekend over what to do about her disappointing pay raise before deciding that a discussion of the matter with Ms. Hopper was the best course to pursue. One of her spontaneous decisions is to apologize to Ms. Hopper for attacking one of the policies supported by the latter. Another is to end the discussion with an agreeable and appreciative tone. These two decisions, it should be clarified, are not the outcomes of full deliberations highly accelerated by some special mental talent of Margaret's. Like the instantaneous decisions of Rachel Hopper or any other rational agent, they are the outcomes of habits of character. More specifically, they result from a disposition not to offend superiors and another to close discussions, at least with superiors, politely and agreeably even when they are not entirely satisfactory. It is quite possible, however, that these habits reflect careful deliberations that occurred much earlier in Margaret's professional life, namely, deliberations about how she should comport herself toward superiors. Habits acquired upon due reflection enable a person to make defensible decisions even when circumstances prevent deliberation.

THE STANDARDS OF MORAL AGENCY

While we have identified the traits of moral agency as they relate to the persons involved in the Margaret Feister case, we have not raised any normative questions specifically related to those features as they appear in the case. We now will pose such questions by considering the significance of the values, rights, and duties of moral agency for the Margaret Feister case.

Freedom

The various persons in the case presumably appreciate freedom, whether that of their respective selves or of one another. The superintendent seems to value the leeway that he has for designing a program to improve instruction in his district. Also, while he imposed a tenure and salary-increase policy upon his principals, he granted them the freedom to construct additional measures for teaching improvement in their respective schools. Rachel Hopper plainly cherishes the opportunity to design and implement such measures, including the hiring of Richard Lopez. She values the liberty of her teachers to inquire about their pay raises. Finally, even though Rachel esteems freedom in her work, she recognizes that her freedom has limits. Thus, she follows the superintendent's policy even though she disagrees with some of it. She also restricts herself from violating Richard Lopez's procedures for instructional improvement.

Without question, Mr. Lopez is pleased to have a wide latitude in developing specific procedures for instructional improvement, and he extended the teachers at Pulaski Elementary freedom to divulge their instructionl problems only as they saw fit. Margaret Feister obviously likes to run her classroom without outside interference. She welcomes the opportunity to discuss her pay raise with her principal even though she will have to talk about her teaching, which usually she does not want to do. In both situations, however, she tends to impose limits to her freedom. She has what she considers to be good reasons for her teaching. She shows concern that her feelings might overwhelm her discussion with Ms. Hopper. In apologizing for direct criticism of a measure followed by Ms. Hopper, Margaret tries to keep from offending her.

Even though it is more or less evident that these persons like their freedom, it is not fully clear why they like it and what respect they have for one another's freedom. Does the superintendent prize his liberty because it is something he ought to have as a moral agent in his situation or because he sees it only as an opportunity to advance his career? Does he extend freedom to his principals because he regards them as competent and responsible or because he is afraid of displaying his ignorance about instructional improvement? Would the superintendent be content without the freedom to construct his own program as long as the absence of that freedom did not imperil his career advancement? Would he take over the evaluation of the teachers of individual schools if he thought he could do so without hurting his career chances? Does he feel obligated to establish conditions in the Lincoln School District that will sustain and nourish the liberty that is morally appropriate to himself in his specific situation as well as the liberty that is morally appropriate to his principals and teachers in their specific situations?

Even though Rachel Hopper's appreciation of liberty does not appear to be problematic, Richard Lopez's does. We have no reason to suspect that Mr. Lopez esteems his freedom for selfish reasons, but we do have some ground to wonder about the liberty he has extended the teachers of Pulaski Elementary. He regards the liberty, we know, at least partly for instrumental reasons: He believes that permitting the teachers to be the ones to identify their major instructional problems will encourage them to trust him and thus his efforts at instructional improvement. But does he view that freedom as belonging to the teachers only because he has given it to them, or does he see it as something that morally pertains to them, as something to which they have a moral right and thus which he morally must respect? On the other hand, does he believe that because of pedagogical incompetence they do not yet have that liberty as a moral right and that until they earn it as a moral right they should have it only as he grants it to them for tactical reasons?

Despite her pride as a teacher, Margaret Feister apparently sees her freedom as an opportunity not for ego gratification but rather for teaching well, at least as measured by her standards of good teaching. Even her liberty to discuss her pay raise with Rachel Hopper is taken by her as a chance to learn how and where her teaching has fallen short. Indeed, we suspect that her hurt pride has arisen as much from the prospect of having disappointed herself in her teaching as from resentment of Ms. Hopper's not fully appreciating her teaching. Nevertheless, there are some troubling aspects to her freedom. She refuses to share her specific pedagogical experiences with other teachers; she works passively and reluctantly on the instructional improvement committee; and she declines to be forthcoming with Mr. Lopez. In taking the liberty not to do these things, Ms. Feister, in effect, places obstacles in the ways of her colleagues and Mr. Lopez to gain knowledge about her teaching that might help improve instruction in Pulaski Elementary. Does she have the right to create these obstacles? Are her colleagues and Mr. Lopez really so incompetent that they cannot comprehend and benefit from her pedagogical experience? Perhaps her colleagues and Mr. Lopez have the right to learn about her pedagogical experience. Perhaps she is obligated to reveal these experiences as a way of bettering instruction at Pulaski Elementary.

Knowledge

Questions about the superintendent's view of knowledge abound. Does he so appreciate the place of knowledge in action that he has attempted to become highly informed about instructional improvement in general and about the conditions in the Lincoln School District specifically related to instruction? Does he believe that two classroom observations per year are sufficient for learning about a teacher's instruction? Has he considered that he might have the duty to establish and foster practices in the Lincoln district that will encourage the acquisition of knowledge about instruction not only by administrators but also by teachers? Is he prepared to use systematically the knowledge that his principals gain about their teachers as part of a comprehensive effort to develop teaching in the district, or will he use it only as occasions compel him to?

The knowledge involved in Rachel Hopper's activities entails several issues. While there is no question that Ms. Hopper has obtained facts about the instruction of her teachers, there is a concern as to whether or not she has obtained enough facts to make judgments about the quality of that instruction. There is the further question as to whether or not she can infer from facts about a teacher's instruction obtained under formal conditions of observation to what that teaching is regularly like. There also is an issue about method. The only systematic way that Ms. Hopper has for acquiring knowledge about her teachers' instruction is the classroom observations prescribed by the superintendent. Supplemental ways are discussions with teachers and with Richard Lopez. As noted earlier, the classroom observations are too restricted to be fully reliable, and the discussions are too incidental and scattered to provide comprehensive information. We wonder, then, if there are other methods that are more reliable and, at the same time, do not threaten the moral rights and duties that Ms. Hopper's teachers and Richard Lopez have as educators.

Because Richard Lopez has decided to place a premium upon establishing trust between himself and Pulaski Elementary School's teachers, he has decided further to rely entirely upon self-reports by the teachers on what their major instructional problems are. Accordingly, it is open as to what knowledge Mr. Lopez actually has about those problems. While he has knowledge about what the teachers willfully say their major instructional problems are, he thereby does not necessarily have knowledge about what those problems really are. Despite Mr. Lopez's good faith efforts, some teachers, being cautious about administrators, might not want to disclose their serious problems. Others might confuse major problems with minor ones. Perhaps Mr. Lopez intends to rely upon the teachers' self-reports only until he has gained the confidence of the teachers and means to institute a new way of learning about their instructional problems. What method will that be? Even if a new method does not weaken the trust already established, how can it be designed so as not to be unduly authoritarian or intrusive?

Margaret Feister's knowledge about her teaching derives mainly from conscientious reflection and to a much lesser extent from her discussion with Rachel Hopper. That Ms. Feister does not share this knowledge with her colleagues raises a question about her moral duty as a teacher. Because any moral agent has the obligation to promote conditions supportive of knowledge and the other features of moral agency, does not Ms. Feister have the duty to share her knowledge about teaching with her colleagues so as to help improve instruction at Pulaski Elementary? Moreover, that she does not try to gain insights about teaching from colleagues also raises the issue of whether or not she has defensibly discounted her colleagues as a possible source of such insights. As she heard from Ms. Hopper, she is not the only good teacher at Pulaski Elementary, and if she had listened to others, she might have learned something useful about how to have all students regularly participating together in class. Finally, because Margaret Feister is dissatisfied about Ms. Hopper's knowledge of her classroom instruction, is she obligated to help her principal gain more knowledge about her instruction? After all, as a moral agent Margaret has some duty to cooperate in establishing knowledge about her teaching. Despite the superintendent's connection of tenure and merit pay with the rating of instructors, the ultimate point of the rating is to improve instruction. As a teacher, then, does not Margaret have a duty to help in the rating of her own instruction especially when that rating cannot be reliably performed without her cooperation?

Purpose and Judgment

The purposefulness in the Margaret Feister case involves three kinds of issues: conflict, vagueness, and revision. As already suggested, uncertainty about the full intentions of the superintendent prompts us to wonder about the possibility of a clash between his prudential interests and those he should have as an educator. Is he seeking career security or advancement at the expense of his obligations as a superintendent? If he is, then he is acting contrary to the demands of moral agency, which are superior to those of prudence. The policy of seeking instructional improvement through making tenure and salary decisions on the basis of instructional evaluation poses the strong possibility of internal conflict. While the policy purports to use tenure and salary decisions as a means for improving instruction, it also sends the message that the reverse is true, that good teaching is a means for obtaining tenure and salary increases. Because teachers might see instructional evaluations involved in such decisions mainly as means for making those decisions, they might regard the evaluations primarily as threats to their welfare or as chances to impress evaluators rather than as opportunities to alter their instruction for the benefit of students.

While Richard Lopez has designed his program of instructional supervision with the goal in mind of establishing trust between himself and the teachers with whom he works, he presumably takes that goal to be not an end in itself but ultimately a condition for improving their instruction. The difficulty is that his idea of what will count in the long run as instructional improvement is vague. Thus, it is not clear what he will do with the trust the teachers might place in him eventually. Unless he develops a clear idea of what he will do with it, he runs the risk of transforming it into just a "feel good" rapport with teachers, thus wasting his opportunity to improve their instruction.

Probably no one would accuse Margaret Feister of pursuing personal gain over professional service, but we might wonder about the goal she sets for herself as a teacher, namely, to prepare her students for their next grade level. The difficulty here is that the purpose is somewhat vague. What precisely is expected of her students at their next level?

Presumably some academic competence and social development are expected, but exactly what they are is not evident. Moreover, who defines these expectations: Margaret Feister, the teachers of the next grade level, the curriculum director of the school district? Ms. Feister appears to regard the expectations as chiefly academic. But if she actually does regard them as such, is she justified in her view? Maybe not. Rachel Hopper's stress upon the social development of students indicates that the social might be just as important as the academic. Moreover, it is not evident that when Margaret leaves Ms. Hopper's office she will revise her instructional purpose on the basis of what she has learned from Ms. Hopper. Given Margaret's deep pride, we should not be surprised if she did not alter her purpose. Even so, is she not bound at least to reconsider her purpose in order to determine whether or not it needs modification?

Moral agents choose their purposes, we have explained, on the basis of judgments. Hence, because there are issues related to the purposes of the agents in the Margaret Feister case, there might be issues related as well to the judgments underlying their purposes. One question bears on the standards by which the superintendent chooses his purposes. Does he choose goals according to their educational worth or according to their importance for his career? Because he might be favoring the prudential over the moral, he needs to reflect upon his character and, if necessary, to improve its moral quality. Another issue relates to norms for Richard Lopez's future instructional evaluation. Once he has gained the confidence of Pulaski's teachers and thus no longer must rely upon teachers' self-reports, what standards will he use to judge the quality of instruction? Finally, there is a question about the criteria by which Margaret Feister judges her instructional purposes. More specifically, should not those criteria be broader so as to include nonacademic aspects of student performance?

Decision and Deliberation

That the superintendent needs to reflect upon his character suggests also that he needs to reconsider the policy decisions that he made on instructional improvement. Did he make those decisions mainly because they were the best ones available for improving instruction in the Lincoln School District or chiefly because they would protect his career? Did he make those decisions with adequate knowledge about instructional improvement, or did he make them while somewhat ignorant about the matter? But the superintendent's examination of these questions presupposes his entertaining them, and under what conditions he is likely to think about them is a crucial question, too.

The standards that Rachel Hopper uses in deliberating and making decisions might not be perfect in all respects, but they seem to be mainly sound. They tend to favor the benefit of the student; moreover, they are subject to critical review by Ms. Hopper. Even though some of Ms. Hopper's judgments of instructional quality have to be made on the basis of incomplete knowledge, they are not thereby hopelessly faulty. Not only is Ms. Hopper open to reflection on her own judgments and decisions, but she also is disposed to seek the knowledge that she lacks. While Richard Lopez is in no danger of confusing prudential norms with moral ones, he has not yet mentioned to Ms. Hopper what the next step in his instructional improvement program will be. Yet, we sense that Mr. Lopez, either on his own or through interaction with Ms. Hopper, eventually will recognize that he needs to deliberate on how to apply that conception to Pulaski's classrooms.

While Margaret Feister makes decisions on the basis of norms that she sincerely believes to favor the educational benefit of students, she appears not to have examined those standards thoroughly, especially as they apply to the development of students in nonacademic facets. Moreover, at the same time that she is willing, somewhat reluctantly, to discuss the norms with Ms. Hopper, she is rather defensive about them. Despite her willingness to discuss them with Ms. Hopper, Margaret is not inclined to talk about them with others, including her colleagues and Mr. Lopez, her instructional supervisor. This reluctance to engage in conversation about her instructional norms runs parallel to her refusal to use her colleagues and Mr. Lopez as possible sources of knowledge about her students and teaching methods. In short, Margaret suffers a serious character defect; she is not sufficiently open to self-criticism.

CONCLUSIONS

In view of the foregoing analysis, we can draw several conclusions about the Margaret Feister case. They are prescriptions regarding the features of moral agency as they pertain to all or just some of the involved parties.

1. The superintendent and Richard Lopez need to understand that freedom is a quality that belongs to educators as moral agents and not just an instrumentality to be extended to or removed from educators

for the sake of effectiveness. These two individuals may take advantage of freedom as a means for attaining ends, but they should not treat it as just a means. Rachel Hopper and Margaret Feister, despite their differences, appear to regard freedom as a moral right of educators.

2. Margaret Feister must help her colleagues to improve their instruction. Any right of any moral agent poses duties upon others. At the very least, it obligates others not to interfere with that agent's exercise of that right. But it also might bind them to render assistance to that agent in the exercise of that right. The right of the teachers at Pulaski Elementary School to improve their instruction obligates Margaret Feister to help them where she reasonably can. Some of her colleagues need to improve their teaching, and she is a person who might be able to help them to that end. However, by refusing to talk with them individually about her teaching, by refusing to discuss her teaching with Richard Lopez, and by working passively as a member of the instructional improvement committee, Margaret in effect declines to assist them in their efforts. Because Rachel Hopper and Margaret have talked about her instruction, perhaps Ms. Hopper should try to lead Margaret to see that she has a duty to help.

3. The superintendent must be sure that his program for instructional improvement is grounded on all relevant knowledge that he can obtain. Because he is not especially well informed about the improvement of teaching, he must rely upon the expertise of others. It is not clear, however, that he has relied upon any expertise or, if he has, that the knowledge obtained through it is complete. Perhaps the superintendent should appoint a district committee to review pertinent literature and the first year of his policy's operation to determine where and what kind of knowledge is lacking. The instructional evalauations by the principals are some of the data that such a committee should consider.

4. Rachel Hopper should continue trying to identify morally acceptable ways to gather needed information about the instructional performance of Margaret Feister and other teachers. She plainly senses that spying on teachers reflects a condition of distrust between them and her, which in turn indicates that they and she do not respect one another as moral agents. Nevertheless, she is stumped on how to proceed in a morally acceptable way to learn more about Margaret's performance. It might be that she will be unable to do this without Margaret's cooperation. Maybe, then, she should consider observing Margaret, beyond the two required sessions, at Margaret's invitation. As confident

as Margaret is in her own abilities, she should not be afraid to invite Ms. Hopper to observe her at a mutually agreeable time. To be fair to all other teachers, however, Ms. Hopper should provide them with the opportunity for invited observations. When she does acquire additional knowledge about Margaret's or some other teacher's performance, she should use the knowledge in a review of any previous judgment about that performance.

5. Richard Lopez has to determine a way to identify instructional problems at Pulaski Elementary School other than self-reporting by the teachers. While this way must respect the teachers as moral agents, it also should not undermine the trust that he has established with them. One way is suggested by our proposal that instructors might invite Rachel Hopper to observe them in their classrooms. More specifically, Richard Lopez might encourage teachers to invite him into their classrooms to make exploratory observations. While he would retain, so as to keep the faculty's trust, the practice of identifying instructional problems through self-reporting by teachers, he would compare, in conferences with teachers, his exploratory observations with their self-reports of instructional problems. Thereby, he and the instructors could reach a mutual understanding of what their problems are.

6. The superintendent should clearly recognize that the primary goal of his efforts at instructional improvement is better teaching in the Lincoln School District, not the advancement of his career. If he already firmly grasps this goal, he behaves in ways suggesting at times that he regards his policy on instructional improvement mainly as a ticket to an enhanced career position. But if he is confused about the central purpose of the policy, it is problematic as to how he might acquire insight into the purpose. After all, which subordinate would tell the superintendent that he has his priorities mixed up? Which board member would have enough knowledge of the superintendent's mind and policy to detect where his priorties lay? It might be that Rachel Hopper and others who will have input into revisions of the policy will have the best opportunity for influencing his thinking on the matter. Some of their proposed revisions might be perfectly defensible from the standpoint of instructional improvement but might be objection-able to the superintendent from the standpoint of his career. For instance, he might not want to ask the school board for increased spending on staff development; he might not want to dismiss the teachers found to be incompetent. When Ms. Hopper and others find the superintendent objecting to perfectly reasonable proposals, they

will have, and should take, the opportunity to remind him of the fact that he is on record as committed to instructional improvement. If they, then, learn that he refuses to honor his commitment, they will know that he is more concerned with something else, perhaps his relationship with the school board. Moreover, they will recognize that they will have to continue working toward instructional improvement in their schools with less than solid support from the superintendent.

7. The superintendent, Rachel Hopper, and the others responsible for instructional improvement in the Lincoln School District should rethink the relationship between the use of instructional evaluation for making tenure and salary decisions and its use for helping classroom teachers with their classroom problems. While the superintendent appears to believe that the rating of teachers for tenure and salary decisions will eliminate incompetent teachers and encourage others to improve their performance, he seems oblivious to the possibility that this rating will threaten evaluations by instructional supervisors. While Rachel Hopper and Richard Lopez apparently believe that the two kinds of evaluation need not be in conflict, they have encountered difficulties in keeping the rating of teachers from interfering with the instructional supervision of the teachers.

Those who shape policy on instructional improvement in the Lincoln district need to consider several questions: Does basing tenure and salary decisions on ratings of instructors significantly improve classroom teaching? If so, can such ratings be done without violating the values, rights, and duties of teachers as moral agents? Also, if the rating of teachers is effective, does it make instructional supervision unnecessary? If it does not, can either approach to instructional improvement be designed so as not to violate the values, rights, and duties of teachers as moral agents? Can the two approaches co-exist without violating the integrity of instructors as moral agents? On the other hand, even if the evaluation of instructors for tenure and salary decisions does make instructional supervision unnecessary, that kind of evaluation is not necessarily preferable to instructional supervision as an approach to instructional improvement. Which, then, is more respectful of teachers as moral agents?

8. If Richard Lopez is to continue with instructional supervision, he must, in consultation with Rachel Hopper, articulate defensible criteria of good instruction and construct a program of instructional improvement based on those criteria. Only when he has such a program in mind

will he be in a position to make judgments and recommendations independent of the self-reports of teachers.

9. Because Margaret Feister has learned that at least some aspects of her teaching performance have been seriously questioned by her principal, she ought to reflect upon her instructional goals and methods, including the standards underlying them. Reflection by her does not necessarily mean that she will find anything that will need changing. However, because she is inclined to rely mainly upon her own appraisals of her teaching, she will not be in a position to know if anything about it requires changing unless she does seriously review it. To help ensure that she looks at her teaching in a fresh way, she will do well to discuss it with Rachel Hopper further or with Richard Lopez or with other teachers. That she will ever talk about her instruction with Mr. Lopez or her colleagues presupposes that she will have to become less prideful. This change in character might be encouraged by Rachel Hopper, who not only has tact but also seems to have gained, because of her displayed understanding of instruction, some professional respect from Margaret.

6

Curriculum Reform in Occupational Studies

The world of work is a major part of life, at least for most of us. Sometime during the first two or three decades of our lives, we usually acquire knowledge, skills, and attitudes for performing jobs, which may be blue collar, professional, domestic, clerical, technological, or some other kind. We typically spend the next three decades or so doing our work and think of that time as the peak period of our existence, speaking of our later years as retirement from work, as a well-earned rest, or as a period of declining years. This pattern holds whether our jobs are onerous, dull, and unfulfilling or challenging, exciting, and materially rewarding. It is not surprising then that many people regard the world of work as *the* major sector of human life.

The American public schools historically have done well in preparing the nation's youth for semiskilled and skilled occupations and for advanced studies leading to professional careers. Indeed, during much of the twentieth century, education at those schools has been viewed as a vehicle headed toward a good job. To be sure, trade and industrial education in the public schools has had problems. It often has been treated as a dumping ground for academically inferior students. It occasionally has taught students obsolete skills. It sometimes has employed teachers with suspect qualifications. Finally, it frequently has failed to establish employment opportunites for students who have wanted to enter the workplace upon graduation. As serious as these problems have been, however, they have not kept the public schools from helping to foster most of the talent for operating the nation's economy, which has been the world's most successful.

Regardless of how effective the public schools have been in occupational studies in the past, they face new difficulties now and for the future. The first problem concerns the location of jobs. Because the economies of the world's nations are becoming enmeshed with one another to form a global economy, they increasingly are eliminating national barriers to the job market. Hence, America's schools can no longer think of vocational education for just a national economy. The second problem relates to the rapid rise of automation, which steadily has abolished types of occupations. This means that vocational education must help prepare students to be ready to change careers several times during their working lives. The third problem is that many new routine jobs will be in the area of computer technology. Accordingly, schools must devise ways to teach technical skills with expensive equipment to the vast majority of their students. The fourth problem is that a significantly large number of students are not inclined to learn to become members of the workforce. Hence, schools have to determine what they can do to guide those students to become positively interested in the world of work.

THE SITUATION AT MARCUS GREIS
HIGH SCHOOL

Marcus Greis High School is the oldest secondary institution in the Weirton Independent School District. It opened several years before World War I began, when Weirton started to thrive as an industrial center and attract an immigrant workforce. At that time, the school's curriculum was predominantly academic, with just a smattering of practical subjects. Most of the school's 500 students, largely male, planned to attend college and have professional careers; the rest hoped that their high school studies would lead to white-collar positions of some kind. The vast majority of students in Weirton quit school after the eighth grade and sought employment in the city's industries. They typically took unskilled work, learning skills on the job as needed.

During World War I and the 1920s, Weirton prospered along with much of the rest of America. An increase in the city's compulsory school-attendance age caused a large increase in enrollment. Many of the new students at Marcus Greis, including females, had no interest in going to college. To accommodate these students, the school greatly expanded its range of studies. The new courses were in citizenship and performing arts but also in home economics, trade and industrial education, and business. Later, during the Great Depression, the school's curriculum added distributive education, which prepared students for jobs in shops, groceries, and other retail businesses. After midcentury, the number of Marcus Greis students taking the college preparatory program increased significantly, but the majority of the school's students remained interested in coursework leading to blue-collar and clerical jobs upon graduation. Some of the latter students attended, after graduation, the state-sponsored technical school in the Weirton area, which offered advanced training in electronics repair, traditional skilled trades, medical technology, and middle-level commercial positions.

In the past two decades, the city of Weirton has undergone changes that have seriously influenced its schools, especially Marcus Greis. Enormous increases in America's energy prices, foreign competition, the development of high technology, and expensive capital caused many of the city's businesses to go under, relocate, and reorganize with smaller and cheaper workforces. These changes in turn led to a departure of residents, a drop in living standards, an increase in the number of people depending upon public assistance, and a decline in the city's tax base. Not only did financial support for Weirton's schools decline, but the composition of the student body radically changed. Children of immigrants newly arrived from Asia and Latin America replaced fourth-generation descendants of European immigrants. Students with parents alienated from public schooling replaced students from families with a faith in its benefits. Students with unemployed single parents replaced students from families with two working parents. Discipline problems became difficult; academic performance dropped; and the drop-out rate jumped.

Marcus Greis responded to these changes in various ways. At first, the school did very little. Then, under the prodding of both national and state reform efforts, it took measures to strengthen its academic standards; introduce its students to computer technology; and provide courses dealing with drugs, sex, and "core values." These measures did not significantly improve conditions at Marcus Greis even after ten years, but they did not make them worse either. The long-time principal was content to await further orders from above and deal with whatever problems erupted at the school. Two years ago, however, that principal announced his retirement. The superintendent and school board moved to hire a principal who would work hard at improving Marcus Greis in important ways.

THE CASE OF THE OCCUPATIONAL STUDIES CURRICULUM COMMITTEE

The new principal, Mr. George Andrews, soon moved to revamp several programs in the Marcus Greis curriculum, including that of Occupational Studies. Deciding that a special committee was needed to work on that program, he made Henry Bridger, the head of the department of Occupational Studies, the chair of the committee. He also appointed to the committee Karla Jensen, a teacher of computer technology; James Choi, a teacher of English; Reba Burkes, a teacher of mathematics; and Stephanie Stepanic, the assistant principal for instruction.

None of the teachers was enthusiastic about being on another committee. They regarded their instructional loads as full time; they knew that committee meetings would occur after regular school hours; and they sensed that the committee work would be demanding. Nevertheless, they believed that the Occupational Studies program had major problems. They also recognized that the principal's support of curricular reform gave them a rare opportunity to make meaningful changes in the program. So, while they were not eager to serve on the Occupational Studies Curriculum Committee, they quietly anticipated that the task would prove worthwhile.

After closing the door to the conference room, Henry Bridger opened the first meeting with an overview of the committee's mission. "As you probably know, the principal wants us to rethink the Occupational Studies program. It has been nearly ten years since serious changes were made in it, and lots of developments in business and industry have happened during that time. The principal wants us to consider at least three modifications. First, he wants us to figure out ways to link Occupational Studies with the academic areas of the school. He believes that the program can benefit from closer ties with academics. Second, he wants us to make the program more meaningful to the students. He thinks that many students who drop out would stay in school if they found Occupational Studies more relevant or interesting.

Finally, he hopes we will find some way to establish more direct ties with business and industry around Weirton so that our graduates will have a greater assurance of jobs when they finish school. There are other points this committee might want to examine, and the principal said we should feel free to take them up. Okay, I am done talking. Who has a suggestion on how we might deal with any of the principal's charges?"

After a few moments of routine quick glances and paper shuffling by the committee members, Reba Burkes began the discussion. "I suppose that closer ties between the Math Department and Occupational Studies can be had, but it isn't clear to me just what direction we should take. A long time ago Voc Ed students took something called 'general math,' but they quit doing that when the world decided everybody needed algebra. Should the students in Occupational Studies now go back to general math or try something else? Any clues, Henry?"

"Not a one at the moment, at least. Maybe Mr. Choi has some ideas."

"As you know," James Choi began, "I have been at Marcus Greis for only a few years, so I don't know much about the school's past. But it is my impression that vocational education students in many places used to take English courses like the general math ones. In fact, they might have been called 'general English.' Also, there used to be courses called 'business English.' There was a public perception, I believe, that such courses in English and math had inferior content. Students taking them always performed poorly on standardized tests. Of course, many students in Marcus Greis now do poorly on those tests even though they are taking traditional math and English courses."

"May I say something on this?" Karla Jensen asked rhetorically. "Many of the Occupational Studies students go through my classes, and they express their feelings to me from time to time. One thing they say is that they like their math and English teachers but they do not understand why they should have to take algebra and learn all the rules of grammar. But they also recognize that computers are important for them in this day and age. So maybe we should think about using computers in teaching math and English and science and history, too. That way, the students might not see their academic subjects as just so many old hoops they have to jump through to get a diploma."

"What a coincidental idea," said Stephanie Stepanic. "In fact, I recently read an article about a similar thing in other cities. It might even be that all our students—not just those in Occupational Studies—should study all their courses through computer technology. Either way, however, we will have to consider where the computers and programs will come from and whether or not the faculty is prepared to use them if we get them. What do you think, Henry"

Mr. Bridger carefully wiped his glasses with his handkerchief. "Well, just about all the teachers in my department can do computer instruction, and I suspect that most of those in science and math can do it too. I have no notion of what the situation is in other departments. It might be, however, that before we go any further in this vein, we need to ask if computer instruction is going to make school any more attractive to those students who are likely to drop out in the foreseeable future. I am aware that those students see their academic courses as irrelevant, but I also know that they do not care much for their courses in Occupational Studies either."

"You've got something there," interjected Ms. Burkes. "I've noticed that the students who complain about algebra are fairly good ones. They're not the best by a long shot, but they will struggle with the subject. Those likely to drop out don't try, and most of them don't even bother to complain about how useless algebra is. I sometimes wonder how they think they can get a job and stay out of trouble without some kind of high school education."

Mr. Choi had heard Ms. Burkes and other teachers make similar comments before. While he agreed with the general tenor of their remarks, he thought that they overlooked a point. "Perhaps we are taking too much for granted. It might be that our at-risk students simply are not interested in careers. They might see them as alien. From what I have read in sociological studies, I believe students at risk relate to street life, not to the workplace. Street life gives them role models; it gives them peer respect; and it provides them with instant gratification even if through illegal means. It does not ask them to look up to adults, to work hard, save, and plan for the always distant future. In their eyes, then, work is for chumps."

Ms. Stepanic managed to suppress an expression of dismay. "James, that is a very insightful point. I had never thought of the matter in exactly that way. But it paints a gloomy picture for us, don't you think? I mean, half or more of the students in the vocational program here probably won't finish school. And if they don't see anything in the job market with which to identify, then there is nothing we can do to make Occupational Studies relevant to them. Is that how you see it, James?"

"Not exactly, Ms. Stepanic," he replied. "What the point implies, I believe, is that changes in the curriculum in Occupational Studies or any other program at Marcus Greis are not enough to reach the students we have been talking about. Those changes might appeal to students already committed to career preparation, but they just won't turn at-risk students around. To do something for those students, we would have to alter their culture, their social situation. And somebody would have to begin working with them long before they arrive at Marcus Greis. Actually, I don't even know that a school is the right institution for trying to bring about such changes. We do not have any control over the families and neighborhoods of our students."

Henry Bridger stirred in his chair. "Stephanie, I believe that James is right. We need to recognize that the outlook on life by students at risk largely influences how they react to school programs. Also, I have to admit that I don't see that this or any other school has enough impact upon its students' families and their ways of life to get at-risk students to see work as an opportunity for a good life. From talks I have had with our principal, I believe that he too recognizes these things. But neither of us thinks our task is hopeless. Even if we cannot turn around the potential drop-out students as a group, we can reach individuals among them. Nobody expects us to perform miracles. So, rather than giving up on these students altogether or waiting for a social revolution, we need to be thinking about how we can do something for at least some of them."

Ms. Burkes looked up from the doodle she had been making on her tablet. "Henry, that makes a lot of sense to me. But before I go any further, I'd like to hear what James thinks about it. He was the one to raise the problem."

Mr. Choi smiled. "That's true, Reba. But it's much easier to raise problems than to find solutions to them. Fortunately, we have Mr. Bridger leading our committee. His common sense has helped me see through the fog brought on by my limited reading in sociology. Maybe I'd better stick to poetry and novels in the future. At any rate, his idea for focusing on individuals rather than groups sounds good."

"Okay," Ms. Burkes resumed. "If we are to deal with individuals, then we have to find out which ones are interested in pursuing a line of work, not idleness and crime. I don't just mean asking them to raise their hands if they want to have a job when they leave school. Hand raising will identify some students, but it won't identify those in the at-risk category. Students in that group who are interested in jobs might not admit to it in public because of peer pressure. What we might need will be counselors who will privately interview all students in Occupational Studies to find out if they have a vocational interest."

"That's right," said Ms. Stepanic. "But those individual students are going to need a support system in all their course work. There is peer pressure in English and math classes, not just Occupational Studies. Occupational Studies and the academic departments will need to work with each other so that all instructors are aware of which students are committed to pursuing jobs. This is done for other students with special interests and talents, for instance, in science, music, and athletics. Maybe we can do it for individuals in Occupational Studies without putting them on the spot and without slighting other students."

Mr. Bridger cleared his throat. "I think you people have brought forth some good suggestions, but I want to remind you that we will be meeting again, and probably more than once again. So we don't have to work out details of proposals at this time. Also, we want to be sure to take up the third matter that the principal wants considered, namely, how to create more school-to-work ties."

The committee members became quiet while they shifted their attention to the new issue. Ms. Jensen broke the silence. "One thing we should consider is an apprenticeship program. We could locate various industries in the Weirton area who are willing to provide supervised entry level work on a part-time basis. The primary purpose of the program would be exploratory. That is, students who think they might want to work in, say, the health field could have a chance to work as apprentice nurses to see if they really do like that field. They would be juniors and seniors, and they would have a chance to work themselves into a full-time position upon graduation. Distributive education already does something like this, but its program aims at retail businesses. The one I have in mind would aim elsewhere."

Ms. Stepanic was enthusiastic. "That idea sounds like it would make a great contribution, Karla. I really think we ought to follow up on it. There might even be some grant money available for it."

"Yes," Mr. Bridger joined in, "it does sound well worth pursuing. I want to mention a couple of supplemental possibilities, though. It might be possible to develop another apprenticeship program with an emphasis on training. It would not conflict with what Karla has in mind. We could identify industries interested in having apprenticeship trainees, and we could match rising juniors or seniors with industries where they think they would want to have a permanent job. They could complete their course work here on a part-time basis. Another thing we might consider doing is to work out an arrangement with the Weirton technical school so that promising students interested in advanced technical jobs could take training there. That school has all the equipment and staff needed for teaching the skills needed around Weirton."

The other committee members mumbled their approval of Mr. Bridger's suggestions, but nobody had specific comments about them. Then Mr. Choi spoke. "If it is all right, I wish to return to the problem of how to relate academic work to Occupational Studies. It occurred to me just a moment ago that there might be a way of teaching academic courses by orienting them to careers and without sacrificing academic quality. History courses could concentrate on economic matters rather than wars and elections. English could do grammar in a business context and include literature with themes related to work. Science could emphasize the application of science to industry and the consequences of that application for the environment and other aspects of human life. Math could focus algebra and geometry upon real problems from the workplace. The present faculty should be able to teach such courses. We might even think about team teaching between the academic and vocational staffs."

"James," Ms. Stepanic began, "you keep coming up with wonderful ideas this afternoon. I would like us really to keep in mind the notion of putting some vocational content into academic studies. But as Henry has reminded us, we will have time to reflect on it and to develop it in future meetings. There is another problem I want us to think about, too. We have all agreed that the school should work in special ways with those students at risk who have some interest in pursuing careers. But we have not said anything about what the school should do about the at-risk students who do not have that interest. I do not think Mr. Andrews wants those students forgotten or wants us to do any less for them than what we do for other students. So, before we meet again, we must come up with some suggestions on what to do about this problem."

"Thank you, Stephanie," Mr. Bridger said. "We probably have done enough brain storming to get us started. I'll get in touch with all of you soon and ask each of you to follow up on one or two of the recommendations made today. I cannot promise it will be your own recommendation. Those recommendations need different perspectives. But I will make sure that the one you get is one you can handle, at least as well as any of the rest of us. Thanks for your contributions and have a good evening."

IDENTIFICATION OF THE CENTRAL TOPIC

There are two candidates for the central topic of this case. One is the dynamics of the Occupational Studies Curriculum Committee; the other is the committee's discussion of vocational education.

If we take the first option for the theme, we are to focus our attention on the structure and operations of the committee and treat what we learn about vocational education at Marcus Greis as evidence about the committee's structure and operations. There are reasons for assuming this approach. The interplay between the principal and the committee is curious. The academic and vocational membership of the committee poses a potential for conflict. The devotion of the members to their assignment is exemplary. Finally, the effort of the two academic faculty members to help put together a program in Occupational Studies is admirable.

Yet, there also are reasons for concentrating upon the committee's discussion of vocational education. The committee is not just any committee. Its structure and operations are definitely colored by its mission of revising the Occupational Studies curriculum. Moreover, the committee devotes itself to vocational education. Specifically, its members separate the Marcus Greis curriculum into academic and vocational components. They also sort students largely along those lines and subdivide vocational students into those who want to have jobs and those who do not care about having them. Finally, the committee views Weirton mainly as a source of opportunities for work experience and training. In one segment of discussion, the committee verges on expanding its attention from vocational education to the life of work; but it stays on course ultimately by relating that life to vocational education.

It might be that this case includes both committee dynamics and what the committee says about vocational education as core themes. Nevertheless, there are reasons for favoring the committee's discussion over its dynamics. A negative one is that the dynamics are not especially problematic as far as moral agency goes. While the principal's control of the committee is extensive, it does not violate its freedom unduly. The committee's members interact smoothly with each other. In addition, the committee seems fairly productive. A positive reason is that what the committee says about vocational education involves at least one issue of serious moral magnitude. That is the question of what should schools do about students inclined toward street life rather than the workplace.

Accordingly, we shall begin by directing our attention to the opinions that the committee expresses about vocational education. In sum, those opinions are the following: The Department of Occupational Studies can benefit from ties to academic departments, but the reverse is not the case. The students enrolled in Occupational Studies should find the subject meaningful, but many of them will not find it so. Occupational Studies should lead students to jobs. Even students in Occupational Studies who are not interested in the world of work should receive no less attention than those wanting to become a part of that world. If the structure and operations of the committee are germane to the present case, they presumably will emerge as issues in our discussion of these committee beliefs. What we will find is that they do emerge in this way at a few points.

THE TRAITS OF MORAL AGENCY

In order to see what morally important questions might be posed by the views of the Occupational Studies Curriculum Committee, we need to place the committee within the framework of moral agency. To place it there, we will specify the traits of moral agency that are relevant to the beliefs and then show how the norms embedded in those traits apply to the beliefs.

Freedom

According to the comments by the committee's members, freedom is a problematic feature in the life choices of the students at Marcus Greis High School. The students in the college preparatory program presumably are by and large freely there. Even the few students who might be there only because of parental pressure eventually might be thankful that their parents made them go to college. The situation is different, however, for the students in the Occupational Studies program. While roughly half of them probably freely participate in the program, many others are in it simply because they have to be. These are the at-risk students who are inclined to leave school as soon as they are legally old enough and pursue a life on the streets. They are in Occupational Studies because that is where students at risk usually are placed. That these students will freely enter the world of street life is not altogether clear. It might be that social conditioning compels them to seek that life or that threat and intimidation from gang members cause them to seek it. But it also just might be that they find street life more appealing than any other kind of life that is available.

To be sure, according to the committee members, there are at-risk students who presumably will want to be in the Occupational Studies program. Unfortunately, they will find it very difficult at times to act freely in the program. Peer pressure will tend to keep them from pursuing their studies wholeheartedly; indeed, it could discourage some of them from succeeding. Nevertheless, to the extent that they can engage in the program counter to the restraints of their social class characteristics, they can act freely.

Knowledge

Knowledge enters the committee's views on vocational education at several points. While the committee definitely maintains that the Occupational Studies program can benefit from connections with academic programs, it does not even mention the possibility that academics might benefit from connections with Occupational Studies. This should not be surprising. As indicated by our introductory overview of the American high school curriculum in the twentieth century, the traditional position has been that the academic portion of that curriculum is educationally superior to the vocational portion and can improve in no substantial way by association with vocational education. The Committee's silence on this issue, nevertheless, is unfortunate. If the members had entertained the idea that practical experiences related to an area of life as important as work could make sense of academic matters for all students, they would have been in a position to see how to integrate academic and vocational contents in a reciprocal way. They saw how to put vocational meaning into academic studies, but they did not see how to put academic meaning into vocational studies.

Knowledge appears also in the committee's belief that in vocational education even specific occupational knowledge gained in the classroom has to be extensively supplemented by experience and training in the workplace. While this belief has been traditional in the field of vocational education, it might have become less defensible in recent years. Even in Weirton, in an era of automation and rapid economic change, it might be that general and transferable vocational knowledge, for example, pertinent concepts and problem-solving skills, is much more important than the facts and skills specific to one type of job.

Finally, the cognitive feature of moral agency shows up in the committee's view that the Occupational Studies program should work with at-risk students as individuals rather than as a group. Because scientific knowledge about such students, as Mr. Choi came to realize, is about them as a group, it does not provide sufficient information for dealing with each and every member of the group. In the world of educational practice, as Mr. Bridger's common sense indicates, it has to be supplemented with practical knowledge, that is, knowledge of particular members within the group.

Purpose and Judgment

The Occupational Studies Curriculum Committee, neither as a whole nor as individual members, never states the purpose of vocational education for Marcus Greis High School. But it does intimate what it has in mind for that aim: preparation of the school's students to enter the local job market. The point of strenthening the academic quality of the school's vocational program is to make graduates more education-ally respectable and hence more marketable. The point of making the content more interesting to students is to keep them enrolled and hence in a position to learn occupational skills. The point of tying the program to Weirton's economy is not only to help students with career choices but also to help ensure job opportunities upon graduation. The only other goal that might be inferred concerns the committee's remarks about at-risk students: the prevention of crime. That goal, however, is plainly secondary; it is a spin-off of the employment of Marcus Greis students not headed for college. There simply are no allusions to other ends to which vocational education might contribute, such as moral character, religion, aesthetics, private life, and citizenship. We are told how the study of history could help with an understanding of the life of work, but we are not told how occupational studies could contribute to an understanding or appreciation of citizenship.

While preparation for the Weirton job market might seem like a goal based more on tradition than on reflection, it might rest on unspoken reasons, both factual and normative. The factual ones are easy to conceive: The vast majority of students in Occupational Studies prob-ably will live in the Weirton area after graduation. If students are to find employment there, they will have to have knowledge and skills relevant to the area's industries. The normative reason is a value strongly suggested by the committee's members. Thus, when Reba Burkes expresses distress about students who are not at all interested in entering the world of work, she reveals a high valuation of that world. That valuation, however, does not seem to be special only to Ms. Burkes; it appears to be one shared by all other members of the committee. As a matter of fact, the committee applies the lofty status of the life of work not only to students in vocational education but also to students in the college preparatory program. The committee members might believe that the professional careers that the college preparatory students seek will have greater economic and social value than those sought by the other students will have. But what is even more important is that they might believe, albeit silently, that work is a cardinal factor in any worthwhile life. That is, they might be inclined to declare that work organizes and gives social value to a major part of a person's life.

Decision and Deliberation

Deliberativeness occupies much of the committee's discussion. To be sure, there are some things the committee does not get to weigh, and this is one place where the dynamics of the committee emerge as an issue. Not only did Mr. Andrews, the principal, decide a special committee would undertake the revision of the Occupational Studies program and who would serve on the committee and in what capacity. But he also decided what the agenda of the committee should be in the main: Tie the Occupational Studies program to academic fields, make the program's content relevant to students, and establish a close connection with Weirton's industries. While the committee is free to add other items to its agenda, it practically has to devote most of its attention and effort to the principal's measures. Moreover, while the committee's members might or might not favor these proposals, they are in a vulnerable position to challenge them. Finally, the members do not seem to be aware of the reasons lying behind the principal's recommendations. Certainly, neither Ms. Stepanic nor Mr. Bridger, who are the members with the principal's confidence, makes those reasons known. Indeed, none of its members expresses any facts or norms in support of the measures even though they seem to have some in the backs of their minds.

Despite the fact that the committee does not decide upon its agenda, it does have much to weigh in developing the ideas suggested by Mr. Andrews. Nevertheless, in pondering how to develop these ideas, the committee is as remarkable for failing to entertain certain alternatives as it is for specifying some commendable ones. It puts forth computer-assisted instruction and the inclusion of vocational content in academic courses as ways of giving Occupational Studies a stronger academic base, but it ignores altogether the possibility of eliminating subject boundaries and having a widely integrated curriculum, for instance, one organized around the concept of work or a career. The committee considers estimable ways to make Occupational Studies more meaningful to at-risk students interested in entering the work place, but it fails to specify, as Ms. Stepanic mentions, any way to make it meaningful to those at-risk students not interested in pursuing careers. Indeed, it does not raise the possibility of making the curriculum more meaningful for those vocational education students who do not fall in the at-risk category. Morever, even though the committee provides two worthy suggestions on how to connect the Occupational Studies program with the workplace, it assumes that any connections there are chiefly to enable students to make choices among and acquire training for specific careers existing today. It fails to entertain the possibility that students might use those connections as opportunities to help learn how to choose a career not just today but in the future as well, how to transfer general vocational knowledge to specific job situations, and how to discover the general vocational knowledge that is buried in the specific facts and skills of a particular job.

Another glaring gap in the committee's deliberations is the absence of serious attention to reasons by which alternatives are considered. As in the instance of Ms. Jensen's reasons supporting her recommendation for computer-assisted instruction, they typically go without examination by the committee. As examplified by Ms. Stepanic's reference to equal treatment, they tend to be somewhat vague. Finally, as in all instances, they are ad hoc and unsystematically applied. This criticism is no unqualified condemnation of the committee's deliberations. After all, we see it in operation only at its initial meeting, which we might expect to be more of a brainstorming session than a well-organized inquiry. The criticism, rather, is forward looking; it means that the committee in a subsequent meeting should develop and organize good reasons for the alternatives that it wants to adopt.

THE NORMS OF MORAL AGENCY

Having identified the ways in which the traits of moral agency are embedded in what the committee says about vocational educational at Marcus Greis, we now will consider what normative moral questions are prompted by the committee's views. To do that, we look to the values, rights, duties, and virtues of moral agency.

Freedom

Freedom, we noted, relates especially to the at-risk students enrolled in Occupational Studies. Contrary to their group profile, some of those students wish to pursue careers but suffer adverse peer pressure. The others are true to pattern, having negative attitudes toward employment. Indisuputably, the students wanting to pursue careers through the Occupational Studies program have a moral right to do so, and those disinterested in having careers are morally bound not to interfere with the vocational education of those who are interested. Moreover, the teachers and administrators at Marcus Greis, as they seem to recognize, are morally obligated to help those interested in a career deal with the problem of peer pressure. In addition, these teachers and administrators are morally bound to try to correct those students exerting peer pressure.

But what about the freedom of the individual at-risk students who do not care to enter the world of work? Are they free not to enter that world? Do they have a right to pursue some other mode of life? Unfortunately, the answers to both questions have to be qualified.

Students are free to avoid vocations only if they are not made to avoid them. Hence, if the at-risk students of concern are individually determined by their cultural and social backgrounds to avoid careers, then they as individuals are not free not to pursue careers any more than they are free to take up street life. Perhaps some of these individual students are fatally shaped by their background; maybe some of them are not, thus having a capacity to gain control of their lives.

But whether these at-risk students are free or not to reject the life of work, they might not have a right to reject it. Not all employment, we should remember, is morally good or even morally tolerable. For instance, the directorship of a Nazi concentration camp was a morally evil position, neither tolerable nor valuable. Vocations are morally worthy when they encourage the life of moral agency and morally tolerable when they do not undermine that life. More specifically, morally valuable vocations help foster the public conditions of moral agency, further the moral development of its workers, and respect the rights and duties of other moral agents. A morally tolerable career does not weaken the public conditions of moral agency, allows the moral development of its workers, and respects the rights and duties of other moral agents. By these criteria, positions with a government-sponsored lottery appear to be morally tolerable rather than valuable. Even though they probably contribute to the public moral good and respect the moral rights and duties of other agents, they do not encourage, but only allow, moral development in their occupants.

Even if we assume that all the vocations available to Marcus Greis students are morally estimable, we need not conclude that a student morally may never reject them. A student may find them or the Weirton area uninteresting and seek his or her career elsewhere. But what about the at-risk student who prefers the street life to the morally worthy vocational life? Does he or she have a moral right to decline this kind of life and just hang out? Our answer hinges on whether or not his or her hanging out will be morally tolerable at least. Will it help weaken the public conditions of moral agency? Will it deter that individual from developing as a moral agent? Will it impose burdens upon other agents? Unless the street life of an individual in Weirton is remarkably different from what it is elsewhere in America, it in all likelihood will fail these tests. It probably will put a strain upon the public resources needed for moral agency. It probably will hinder the moral development of its participants, and it probably will violate, through criminal activity, the moral rights of many residents of Weirton. In all likelihood, then, an individual student at Marcus Greis High School, at risk or not, does not have a moral right to reject a morally worthy vocational life in preference to the life of the streets. This is so even if the vocational life is not as attractive to the student as is the street world. Likes and dislikes may suffice as good reasons for choosing between two objects of equal moral value, but they are never good reasons for choosing between the moral and the immoral.

Knowledge

Knowledge relates to several points involved in the committee's opinions on vocational education: the superiority of academic to vocational studies, the importance of job-specific knowledge for career exploration and training, and the need to apply scientific research to educational practice with common sense. Academic studies do not necessarily have more educational value than vocational studies have. Both may be educationally valuable, and one of them may be more or less estimable than the other in different situations. In general, academic studies have more educational worth for students with purposes stressing academic qualities whereas Occupational Studies have more educational value for students with purposes emphasizing occupational qualities. Moreover, as we earlier indicated, vocational studies can be useful to academic studies in a way that is similar to the manner in which academic studies can be useful to occupational ones. A possible effect of even implicitly regarding academic programs as educationally superior to a vocational program is that the perception might give the impression that academics is morally, not just educationally, superior to vocational education. This in turn might give the further impression that students in academics must be educationally, perhaps morally, superior to those in Occupational Studies. Consequently, both Mr. Andrews and the committee have to take care not to treat the academic programs at Marcus Greis as necessarily having more educational value than the vocational program.

The committee's inclination to ensure that the students in Occupational Studies learn job-specific knowledge and skills at the expense of general and transferable knowledge and skills may be innocent, but it is certainly questionable from the standpoint of moral agency in this time and place. In the respect that the students learn job-specific competences primarily, they presumably will be less prepared to make new career choices and decisions plus acquire new job competencies than if they also had given equal effort to gaining transferable knowledge and skills. Hence, the committee's inclination is likely to leave the students less prepared to control their lives in the job market and to provide themselves and their dependents with the economic conditions necessary for moral agency.

Finally, while moral agency values scientific knowledge, it also recognizes that such knowledge might apply to practical situations only in approximate ways. Scientific knowledge speaks to general and abstract matters whereas practical knowledge has to address particular and concrete matters, which invariably involve exceptions. Hence, while the Occupational Studies Curriculum Committee should employ social science findings wherever they are relevant to its discussions, it should remain cautious in applying them to Marcus Greis students.

Purpose and Judgment

Even though the Occupational Studies Curriculum Committee never states why the purpose of the curriculum is to prepare students to obtain jobs in the Weirton area, it hints at both factual and normative reasons that support the purpose. The factual ones in sum are that the bulk of occupational students in Marcus Greis will live in or around Weirton. The normative ones boil down to the principle that employment is a major component of a worthy life. Whether considering the committee's factual or normative reasons, however, we find the members remiss. They ignore certain facts, and they are vague in in their conception of a worthy life.

Actually, the committee's neglect of facts is closely related to its vague conception of a worthy life. The only facts seemingly considered by the committee to establish the purpose that it ascribes to the Occupational Studies curriculum are those that answer two questions: Where will the students in Occupational Studies live after they graduate? What knowledge and skills must they learn in order to secure employment? Once the committee assumes that most of the students will live in the Weirton vicinity, it can easily specify the job training necessary for vocational education students at Marcus Greis. Implicit in the committee's thinking, however, is the notion that any semiskilled or skilled position in the Weirton area may be at the core of an estimable life. Whether or not the job may, however, depends upon what the committee takes the characteristics of a valuable life to be. Unfortunately, the committee gives us no more clues to those characteristics than that the life should be within the bounds of the law. Legality is hardly sufficient to qualify a mode of life as morally praiseworthy even if that mode involves skilled work. For example, the life of the governmental functionary is notorious for tedium, narrowness, passivity, and other undesirable qualities.

While the committee fails to clarify what it intends by an estimable life, it should mean a life that is compatible with moral agency. Being moral agents, the students at Marcus Greis are subject to the values, rights, duties, and virtues of such agency. Hence, whatever lives the students pursue ought to agree with those norms; whatever vocations they assume also should be compatible with them. Moreover, because the members of the committee are moral agents with the responsibility of framing ends for students who are moral agents, they are especially obligated to conceive ends that are morally proper for those students. To conceive of a life consistent with moral agency, the committee ought to have employed the features and norms of moral agency as ideas for guiding their discussion of the Occupational Studies curriculum. If it had, it would have been led to consider which sorts of occupations in the Weirton are, as a matter of fact, consistent with moral agency. It would have been prompted to ask the following questions: Which occupations there encourage or hinder freedom, knowledge, purposefulness, judgment, deliberation, and decision making by workers? Which occupations contribute to or undermine health, education, justice, civility, and other public conditions required for moral agency?

Decision and Deliberation

The deliberative quality of the Occupational Studies curriculum, it may be remembered, suffers problems of omission. The first is that the vocational educational curriculum persists in having a departmentalized curriculum. As far as we know, neither the principal nor any member of the committee raises the possibility of having a seriously integrated curriculum. Even though the principal urges the committee to think of a way of establishing a closer link between academic and vocational subjects, the committee approaches the task in an ad hoc way. It goes no further than proposing to infuse some technology into academic courses and using job situations as a source of practical problems in academic courses. The result is that courses will continue to be offered largely on a departmental basis, that the academic sector will retain its status of being educationally superior to the occupational, that students will be separated according to whether or not they aspire to professional careers, and that students not interested in such careers will be ranked, even if only implicitly, as educationally and maybe morally inferior.

If, however, Mr. Andrews and the committee had thought of the students at Marcus Greis as moral agents, they would have recognized that there are topics of generic significance for the lives that all students at Marcus Greis will lead. Take work, for instance. All students need to learn about the importance of work in life as well as the importance of morality in work. They all need to understand what ideas count as morally good reasons for choosing careers. They all need to grasp the point that career choices commit people to long-range moral consequences, many of which are unforeseeable. Finally, they all need to understand that the greater and lesser economic and social values of careers do not impinge upon the equality which people have as moral agents. Hence, the committee would have at least entertained the possibility of organizing much of the Marcus Greis curriculum around themes relevant to the generic practical interests of the school's students.

The committee's attention to making the Occupational Studies curriculum meaningful to those at-risk students interested in having careers is certainly admirable, but its attention should have been directed also toward making that curriculum meaningful to the other at-risk students as well as the vocational students who do not fall in the at-risk category. The committee perhaps assumes that the curriculum cannot be made meaningful to the at-risk students not interested in careers; also, it might assume that the curriculum already is meaningful to those students interested in having careers who are not at risk. If the committee does have these assumptions, however, it needs to articulate and examine them. Are there not some approaches to vocational education for at-risk students that the committee members have not yet come across? Is it not possible to make the Occupational Studies curriculum even more meaningful to those students not at risk who wish to have careers? In any event, both groups of these students should have a meaningful curriculum. Accordingly, they deserve the serious attention of the committee.

Another omission by the committee is a suggestion that the curriculum should prepare students to become flexible in their career choices and to acquire knowledge, skills, and dispositions that are transferable. Since the middle of the twentieth century, we have mentioned, technological and economic conditions have made careers increasingly fluid. This is true of professional as well as nonprofessional positions. From now and into the foreseeable future, students should not assume that their original job training will be the last that they will need and that their initial career choices will be the last ones that they will have to make. They will have to be disposed to retraining from time to time; they will have to be open to several career changes during their working lives. The qualities that students will need to learn for this preparation include respect for knowledge, reflective thinking, purposefulness, deliberativeness, willingness to learn, interpersonal sensitivity, and other virtues of moral agents. If Mr. Andrews and the members of the committee had explicitly formulated an Occupational Studies curriculum within the framework of moral agency, they would have included in it intellectual and affective dispositions that would help its students to adapt to the uncertainties of the newly uncertain world of work.

Finally, the committee fails to articulate the principles by which it does or will decide upon alternatives for the Occupational Studies curriculum. Given our critique of the other omissions by the committee, we submit that its members would do well to use the features and norms of moral agency as basic principles for its decisions. This is not to say that they should employ only these features and norms to guide their deliberations. Economic and educational principles, to name only two other kinds, also have to be used. We wish to point out, however, that the principles of moral agency, being superior to all other kinds of principles, can serve the committee members as principles for screening curriculum alternatives shaped by other kinds of reasons. Even if an option is ecnomically or educationally acceptable, it should not be included in the curriculum unless it is morally acceptable too.

The traits and norms of moral agency may be used by the committee in more than deliberations on curriculum. They also may, and should, be employed as screening principles in the committee's choice of the goal or goals of the Occupational Studies curriculum. If the committee had used these principles in this way, it would have taken measures to ensure that the kinds of jobs in the Weirton area for which students are to be prepared are morally acceptable.

CONCLUSIONS

Several conclusions follow from the preceding analysis. They will be grouped according to the characteristics of moral agency to which they relate. In addition, they will be presented as recommendations for future discussions by the members of the Occupational Studies Curriculum Committee.

1. *Freedom.* The committee is correct in wanting to consider ways to protect from peer pressure the freedom of at-risk students to prepare for vocations. Nevertheless, it also needs to focus on the problematic aspects of the freedom of those at-risk students who show no inclination toward a life of work. To do this, the committee should devise ways to:

a. Deal with these students as individuals rather than as a group. By working with them as individuals, the Marcus Greis staff will be able to identify the particular conditions affecting the freedom of each student. At the same time, the staff will avoid reinforcing the students' undesirable cultural influences.

b. Identify which of these students are completely controlled by their cultural backgrounds and which are partially controlled. This will enable the staff to look for measures that will counter or neutralize adverse cultural factors and those that will build upon freedoms that students already have.

c. Lead these students to comprehend and care about freedom in their lives and in the lives of other people. This curricular content should help students to understand and appreciate, among other things, that they must respect other people's freedom just as they want others to respect theirs, that their free actions may have consequences for which they will be responsible, and that their free actions of today, depending upon their consequences, can stifle or expand the range of their free actions in the future.

d. Help these students to grasp and value the importance of vocations. From a prudential standpoint, students should learn how their jobs and those of other people might benefit themselves. From a moral standpoint, they ought to learn how their jobs might benefit others and society as a whole. Without understanding and esteeming the importance of vocations, students cannot be expected to participate willingly in career education.

2. *Knowledge.* In this category there are three proposals for the committee:

a. The committee should take care to ensure that whatever connections it establishes between academic and vocational studies will be of educational worth to the students in Occupational Studies. At the same time, it should urge Mr. Andrews to consider integrating many of Marcus Greis's courses around vocational and other practically relevant themes.

b. The committee ought to ponder ways of stressing transferrable competences in the content of the Occupational Studies curriculum. Such competences might include practical reasoning, economic principles, and appropriate work attitudes.

c. Rather than being scared away from the social sciences by Mr. Choi's unfortunate example, the committee should seek out more scientific knowledge about at-risk students and the world of work. Even so, it also should acquire more knowledge pertaining to the specifics and particulars of the Weirton area and the students in Occupational Studies. It then will have to apply its scientific information to the Marcus Greis situation in such a manner that it does not disregard the elements that are special, perhaps unique, to the situation.

3. *Purpose and Judgment.* The committee needs to provide an explicit formulation of the purpose of the Occupational Studies curriculum that rests upon a defensible set of facts and norms. The facts may come from the social sciences and from practical knowledge about the Weirton region. The norms may include cultural, social, economic, and educational principles. Whatever they are, however, they must be compatible with the values, rights, duties, and virtues of moral agency. Hence, the members of the committee need to reflect upon the relationships between the world of work and the world of morality. They might initiate an examination of those relationships by asking whether they want to prepare students for any occupations just as long as they are legal or whether they want to ready them for occupations with other worthy qualities. If they assent to the latter alternative, they then might raise the possibility that the occupations of concern will enable students to grow in freedom, knowledge, and social responsibility.

4. *Deliberativeness.* The recommendations in this category follow from omissions on the committee's part. One of the recommendations has importance mainly for the dynamics of the committee, but the other three bear mostly on alternatives that the committee should entertain for the content of the Occupational Studies curriculum.

a. The committee needs to consider seriously the possibility of integrating a substantial part of the Marcus Greis curriculum around themes of practical significance for the school's students. It should weigh, among other possibilities, whether or not the topics should be vocational only, whether or not the integrated sector of the curriculum is to apply to all students or just those in Occupational Studies, whether or not that sector should include core fields only or should include major fields too. If the committee were to look at these and other alternatives from the standpoint of moral agency, it would be disposed toward deciding upon at least a core sector with one or more vocational topics. Such a sector would tend to reinforce a sense of moral equality among students.

b. The committee needs to take up ways for making the Occupational Studies curriculum meaningful to the at-risk students presently uninterested in having careers and more meaningful to non-risk students already interested in pursuing jobs. With respect to the at-risk students, the committee should consider interest inventories of individual students and see which of those interests might be modified so as to favor the world of work. It might find interests that can be redirected by role models and other instances of ex-street people who have taken vocations. It also might discover interests that can be redirected by revelations of the foreseeable consequences of following the street life. With regards to the non-risk students, the committee might succeed by ensuring that the Occupational Studies courses, materials, and equipment are up to date and by including the opportunity for advanced training at the Weirton area technical institute.

c. The committee needs to ponder how to prepare the students in Occupational Studies to become flexible and transferrable in their future careers. As we already have noted, this means that the students must learn more than job-specific competencies. They also must acquire concepts and principles, problem-solving skills, and attitudes that enable them to change and adjust to a variety of job situations. The committee, then, will have to determine in which courses the latter competences are to appear as objectives and content, for instance, academic, vocational, or special. The committee, in addition, will have to decide what is the proper balance between general and specific vocational education.

d. Finally, the committee has to articulate for itself the reasons by which it is to identify and decide upon alternatives for attaining the purpose that it sets for the Occupational Studies curriculum. Some of those reasons, as we previously have suggested, will be educational and economic, but as we also have indicated, the basic ones must be the features and norms of moral agency. The committee might commence an identification of these features and norms if it returns to and probes the assumption about the life of work that it carried into its initial meeting, namely, that that life is greatly preferable to the life of the streets. A thorough examination of that assumption ultimately will have to appeal to freedom; knowledge; interpersonal relations; practical reason; and the values, rights, and duties associated with them. Accordingly, perhaps the first order of business for the committee at its next meeting is to address the claim that work is for chumps.

Rosemont Elementary

During the first half of this century, an American urban public school typically served the students living in the residential area where the school was located. An elementary school drew its students from families living within walking distance of the school; a junior high school drew its students from several nearby elementary school neighborhoods; and a high school's students came from several nearby junior high zones. The residential area was fairly stable, and a family living there frequently had two or more children enrolled in the local schools at one time or another. In general, parents were satisfied with what the schools taught and how they treated their children; they tended to trust and respect teachers and administrators. School friendships often overlapped neighborhood friendships, and classmates spent many years of schooling together. Teachers could obtain intimate knowledge of a student's home life, and parents shared their experiences and impressions of teachers and administrators. Both parents and students thought of their local schools as "theirs." In short, the schools tended to be neigbhorhood schools, not just in location but in practice and feeling as well.

Nowadays, the nation's urban public schools rarely are neighborhood institutions in the serious sense of the term. Many students, living far from their schools, are bused in. Some families in the residential area where a school exists have never had children enrolled in that school. Students frequently are transient, moving on to other areas or other cities every year or so. Families, sometimes having diverse cultural and racial backgrounds, frequently do not share their lives and experiences. A significant number of students have single-parent mothers with a passive interest in schooling. Some parents never even bother to visit the schools attended by their children. Consequently, the schools frequently have no discernible community which they serve. Students often go their separate ways when the school day ends. Teachers have difficulty in meeting parents let alone in learning about the home lives of their students. The people living in a school zone sometimes do not regard it as a neighborhood; they hardly ever think of the school as "theirs."

Nobody seriously wants to return to the neighborhood schools of an earlier time. Those schools, often serving racially or ethnically segregated residential areas, frequently were racially or ethnically segregated. Moreover, the historical conditions that engendered and fostered the stability of the neighborhoods of that era are long gone. Today's economic and social conditions promote frequent change in most places in the nation, especially in the cities. Nevertheless, urban teachers and administrators who have reflected on the matter have to believe that something needs to be done to restore a connection between the schools and the home life of their students. They must sense that curricular reforms, higher standards, instructional development, and improved facilities can have little impact when the dominant forces affecting their students are beyond the control of the schools. On the other hand, many parents probably wish that the schools their children attend were much more influential.

THE SITUATION AT ROSEMONT ELEMENTARY

Rosemont Elementary officially is James E. Higgins Elementary School. It originally got its unofficial tag from the name given, by a real estate developer, to the community area it once served.

Neither Rosemont nor the school, however, still functions as it used to. The area ceased to be a real neighborhood several decades ago. It retains its name only as a convenient means of referring to the strip of apartment buildings, townhouses, clothing stores, cafes, liquor shops, churches, convenience stores, and sundry other buildings lining each side of the two-mile length of Rosemont Boulevard. Few residents have resided in Rosemont as long as ten years; most have lived there less than five. The adults view the area not so much as a home but as a place to live for the time being. While more than half of the residents are African American, a sizable minority is African Caribbean. There also is a cluster from Nigeria. Within these groups, there are subdivisions, some social and some cultural. The African Americans with job and family orientations have only minimal interaction with those dependent on public assistance, and the Caribbeans with a British background have little to do with those with a French or Spanish background. Even though the various groups in Rosemont do not have a common way of life, they are tolerant of each other. Indeed, the only strong negative feelings among the residents is the resentment they share toward the few Asians who have business establishments in Rosemont.

James E. Higgins Elementary continues to be spoken of as Rosemont Elementary only because it sits on Rosemont Boulevard. Three-fifths of its students come by bus from beyond the local area. The majority of these are white; the others are Asian and Mexican. The bussed students, however, are not outsiders to the the students living in the boulevard area. This is because the latter, as well as their parents, have no communal feeling for the school. Like the students from outside the area, they see Rosemont Elementary simply as the place where they have to go to school. They would have no regrets, except for any inconvenience in the arrangement, if they had to attend a school in another part of the city.

Even though Rosemont Elementary has a few bright spots, it is a bad school on the whole. A third of the students do well in their class work, but the others have serious difficulty. The latter, who include about 150 students living in Rosemont, commonly perform two years below grade level in reading and arithmetic. Attempted improvements in the reading and mathematics programs have made no discernible difference. Even though discipline is far from getting out of hand, it is troublesome. Students often talk out of turn and loudly; some use profanity. Running in hallways and pushing in lines occur frequently. Older boys occasionally attempt to fondle girls on the playground. During any year, a dozen or so weapons are confiscated, and a dozen or so students are accused of theft. Stricter rules and punishment have not reduced the misconduct. Despite the efforts of a few parents to keep the parent-teacher organization active, relations between parents and the school generally are weak. Some parents never respond to requests for appointments with teachers or administrators; others never keep their appointments. A few become hostile toward school officials in the course of meetings. The annual Santa Claus play is well attended by parents, whereas the book fairs, science fairs, and fund raisers are not. While most of the teachers try hard each day to help their students learn, they see little progress from year to year. They try from duty rather than hopefulness. The younger ones quietly look for positions in more promising situations.

However, not everybody at the school has given up hope. During her five years as principal of Rosemont Elementary, Elma Kinsly has led the school's faculty in two efforts to improve academic performance and discipline. The first failed, and the second has not been showing success. She, her assistant, and a handful of veteran teachers have remained convinced, nevertheless, that a way can be found to turn the school around. When Ms. Kinsly faces a critical school problem, she usually consults with these people, at least, those who are available for a meeting. Shortly after the beginning of the spring semester of the current year, she scheduled a meeting with her assistant and three of the supportive veteran teachers to start looking again for a way to improve Rosemont Elementary.

THE CASE OF THE SCHOOL COUNCIL

The late-afternoon meeting took place in the principal's office, where a sofa, several chairs, and coffee accommodated everyone. Besides Ms. Kinsly there were Michelle Isaak, a first-grade teacher; Bettye Ervins, third-grade; Estelle Gomez, fifth-grade; and Ernie Girard, the assistant principal and the one who deals with the discipline cases referred to the principal's office.

"Thanks for coming," Ms. Kinsly began. "Your time is precious, and I would not have called this meeting if it were not for something important. About a month ago, I met with people from the superintendent's office about the test scores from late last fall. They represent, you remember, achievement by our students under the program changes we made two years ago. The bottom line is that those scores do not show much improvement. In general, the students who took the test last fall are performing about the same as those who were under the previous program. What this means, of course, is that our current effort has not been any more effective than the earlier one, and we were dissatisfied with its results."

Ms. Kinsly, who had already briefed Ernie Girard on the scores, took a sip of coffee while waiting for the teachers to absorb her information. Estelle Gomez was the first to respond. "Does this also mean that the superintendent's office wants us to make more changes in our academic program?"

"Nobody has said that they want us to," Ms. Kinsly replied. "Actually, the people with whom I talked said that the scores were strictly for our use. Just between you and me, I do not think that the central office knows whether or not our program should be changed. Regardless, what I want to learn from you is what we should do about the scores. Do we accept them as meaning that we cannot improve the performance of our students however we try? Do we take them to mean that we need to revise our program again? Or do we see them as telling us something else?"

For a moment the teachers were quiet. Then Bettye Ervins spoke. "Frankly, I doubt that modifying the curriculum one more time is going to do any good, because I am not as sure as I used to be that the curriculum is the problem. Half the time, I do not have the attention of half my students, and I do not think that I am the only one with that situation. You can have the best curriculum in the world and you will not get good results if your students do not pay attention to what you are teaching them. I really believe that before we go tinkering with our academic program again, we need to do something about conduct."

Ernie Girard looked at Ms. Ervins. "Bettye, I could not agree with you more. In the past three years, we have tightened up the school's discipline regulations. Some of those changes were suggested by the faculty. But I believe we have gotten mixed results at best. More parents than before come to talk to me and teachers about their kids' problems. Yet, we have roughly the same number of incidents that we had before we tightened up. I hate to say this, Bettye, but we might be able to improve classroom conduct only by removing all the misbehaving students from the classrooms. That is not feasible, of course."

"May I say something here?" Michelle Isaak asked. "Maybe we have things backwards. It is true that kids do not learn when they do not pay attention, but maybe they do not pay attention because they are not interested in what we were are teaching them. So, if we made the curriculum more interesting to them, we could get rid of the misbehavior and also get them to learn."

"That might work for a few students," replied Ms. Gomez. "But I think the content of our different grade programs probably is interesting to students. At least, it is developmentally appropriate to almost all of the students. Besides, a lot of our students just do not come from a learning background. When I do get to talk to the parents of poorly performing students, I usually find people who do nothing to help their kids with their assignments. I do not think that one of those children has ever seen a parent reading a book. Rarely do those parents indicate to me that they seriously want their kids to learn. So, while I agree that conduct is important for learning and that an interesting curriculum is important too, we cannot expect students to change their classroom behavior or to become inclined to learning if we do not do something to fill the educational void in their family life."

Mr. Girard put down his coffee cup. "Well, class work certainly is not the only place where family life counts. Some of our parents spank their children to maintain discipline, but we do not. Probably that is a major reason why we have difficulty in correcting the conduct of some students. Other parents are given to rude behavior and that might be another reason why we have trouble in disciplining other students. But even if we cannot control the family situation of our students, we have to do something about their conduct."

After a brief lull in the discussion, Ms. Kinsly decided a summary statement would be helpful. "If I follow what has been said so far, we are not sure what to do about the test scores reported by the superintendent's office. Misbehavior interferes with classroom learning, and family situations detract from learning and conduct too. So perhaps altering the curriculum will be beside the point. But what do we do about misbehavior? What do we do about the deficits in family background?"

"Elma," responded Ms. Ervins, "if I knew what to do about the conduct of just my own students, I would have done it a long time ago. And I certainly do not know what to do about discipline for the school as a whole. Now, as far as filling the family gap goes, I guess that something does need to be done, but I have not the least idea about what to do."

"Look," Mr. Girard began, "maybe we are not the ones who should be making those decisions. At least, maybe we alone should not be making them. We have students with all kinds of backgrounds. Some are familiar to us, but others are not. It is possible that we should be hearing from people who know a lot more about the home life of these kids than we do."

"I do not know whom you have in mind," Ms. Ervins commented, "but I have had little or no luck in getting helpful information from parents. Are you thinking of someone else?"

"Partly, yes. Social workers and ministers who work with the students' families might have useful insights. But I was thinking, too, that some responsible parents might have worthwhile advice. Even residents of Rosemont who do not have children in this school might provide interesting perspectives. Of course, I would want us to include parents from outside Rosemont. The bussed students have their fair share of troubles."

Ms. Kinsly occasionally had heard her assistant express his view on the need for input from parents and others not officially connected with the school system. She thought now would be a good time for him to hear one of her concerns about the view. "Ernie, I have no objection to listening to suggestions by parents and others outside the school. Nevertheless, we are the ones paid by this city to make the decisions on what goes on here, and I do not know that we can transfer that obligation to somebody else."

Ms. Isaak came to Mr. Girard's defense. "Elma, I do not understand Enrie to be saying that we should surrender our decision making to these people. All I hear him saying is that we need to listen to them so that we can be better informed when we make whatever decisions we have to."

"Is that all that you intend, Ernie?"

"Yes, except let me be more specific. We could just listen to information from outsiders, or we could listen to advice in addition to information. I see nothing wrong with the latter alternative. Whether or not their advice would be followed would be our decision, not theirs."

"Listen, Ernie," Ms. Ervins said, "if I were a parent, especially one who had not gone to college, and went to all the trouble to make recommendations at a meeting run by school professionals, I would be very skeptical about their taking me seriously. And if they did not follow my recommendations, I would be put off and find something else to do with my time. If we are to listen to these people to gain insights we do not have, we are committed to taking them seriously. Yet, we should not accept just any recommendation that is made. But I do not know how we are supposed to know which advice of theirs is worth taking and which is not. After all, we are supposed to be largely ignorant on what makes our students behave the way they do."

"It is possible," Ms. Gomez suggested, "that we are forgetting something. We have the authority to run this school because of our professional training and experience, and I believe that our training and experience will enable us to tell a good proposal from a poor one. Also, there is no reason why we have to have those who talk to us to give advice in the way that professional consultants give advice. When you hire consultants, you assume that they are experts and that their recommendations are likely to be good ones. The people we are talking about, however, would not be experts, and we would not be inviting them to tell us what to do. What we are after are suggestions, not advice or formal recommendations, from points of view with which we are unfamiliar. We simply want to find out if we are covering all the bases. If we let those meeting with us know this, we would not set them up for the disappointment that Bettye mentioned."

Ms. Kinsly had another concern about Mr. Girard's idea of hearing suggestions from parents and others. "Ernie, you seem to be getting more insider suggestions for your proposal on outsider suggestions that you bargained for. Anyway, I have another question for you. What kind of administrative structure do you envision for these people. Are they to speak their minds as guests at one or two meetings of faculty and administration, or are they to be regular members of something like a school council?"

"Actually, I lean toward the school council notion," answered Mr. Girard. "The problems we have here are not going to vanish overnight, and any measures we take to address them will have to be under continuous review. My guess, then, is that we will need outsider input as long as our student body is the way it is. So they might as well be regular participants in our discussions on curriculum and discipline."

Ms. Isaak looked up from the tablet on which she was taking notes. "Are you not too optimistic, Ernie, in thinking that outsiders would want to be members of a school council? They might be active for a few meetings, but they are likely to lose interest then. Those coming from outside Rosemont would have to travel ten miles or so to get here. Also, they would have to give up some evenings, which they might not always be able to do. Those living in Rosemont certainly do not have a distance problem, but the parents there might be shy about speaking out in public."

"Those are important points, Michelle, but they can be met. Of the hundreds of parents with students in this school, surely five or six would be willing to be members of a council. And I think that there are ministers, social workers, and business people who are able to serve. As far as shyness goes, we can help work with members on that problem, that is, if it is a problem. Elma probably would see it as a virtue in me."

The last remark drew chuckles from the group. Then Ms. Isaak stated that Ernie had met the points she had just posed but also allowed that another one had just occurred to her. "I do not know how to put this easily, so bear with me. We are talking about inviting some parents and others to give us information and suggestions, right?"

"That is true," replied Mr. Girard.

"So we are treating them as something for our convenience. What I mean is, we do not know enough about our students to make sensible decisions for the school, so we want to invite these people to give us some guidance. If we knew enough about our students to make good decisions, we would not invite these people to participate in a school council, right?"

"I suppose so," said Mr. Girard. "We probably would not need their information and suggestions under those conditions."

"But this is a public school, and America is a democracy. Do not the people have a right to help govern their schools? They pay for them, and it's their kids who attend them."

"Well," Ms. Kinsly said, "we do have school boards, and their members are elected by the people."

"Of course, there is an elected school board for this city. But the board is usually concerned with the district schools in general. I do not think that any body on it is much aware of what happens inside this school. It seems to me that the parents of the students in a school have the right to help shape the rules and curriculum of that school. Maybe residents in the school's surrounding area who are not student parents have that right too."

Ms. Kinsly was puzzled. "So where does this take us, Michelle? Do you mean we cannot invite anybody to serve on a school council?"

"Not exactly, I suppose. What it boils down to is that we should recognize that parents and other so-called 'outsiders' have a right to participate in our school's governance whether we want their help or not."

"Maybe you are right; I just do not know," Ms. Kinsly responded. "I would certainly want to talk with the district's legal officer before we would ever acknowledge that parents and others have this right. The right sounds good in theory, but how sound it is in law is something I do not know. Regardless, we all seem agreed that Ernie's notion of seeking information and advice from parents and others might prove useful. We do not seem agreed, however, on the procedure by which we are to talk with such people. Are they to speak to us as occasional guests, or are they to be regular members of a school council."

"Elma," Ms. Gomez interrupted, "I realize that it is getting late. But I do want to state something about Ernie's school council notion that's bothering me. I will not need more than a minute. We started thinking about getting information and suggestions from parents and others because we do not know enough about our students' families to influence their behavior in school very much. But even if we get all kinds of good information and suggestions at school council meetings, will we then be able to change much about our students? We might find out why they behave the way they do, but will we be able to change them? Their family influence might cancel whatever we try?"

"Gee, Estelle," Mr. Girard replied, "I wish I knew. We should not think of a school council as a magic solution. We want it as a source of information and suggestions and a place for discussion. Whether or not the measures we decide upon will be effective will just have to be seen. Two times before we thought we had solutions only to find out we did not. But I do think that the school council is needed. It certainly will put us in better touch with our students. Also, it might even encourage more parents to think of this school as something with which they can identify."

Ms. Kinsly resumed her effort at closure. "I am glad that we had time for your question, Estelle. Also, I am glad that Ernie was able to answer it. At any rate, it is time to wrap up. When I came to this meeting, I had no idea we would wind up where we did. It is a refreshing outcome. Nevertheless, I want to talk with some other teachers about your suggestions, and I have to find out what the central office's attitude toward a school council is. I will be in touch with you in a week or so."

IDENTIFICATION OF THE CENTRAL TOPIC

At a quick glance, this case appears to involve several major themes. The present-day American urban school is one theme for the reason that virtually everything discussed by Ms. Kinsly and her colleagues relates to such a school. Student conduct is another theme in that it appears in the case as a factor seriously affecting classroom learning. School governance also is a theme for the reason that the group sees it as a means for obtaining insights and sees it further as relating to the rights of parents and others unofficially connected with the school system. Moreover, group process is a theme because of the strong influence the meeting, which is quite informal, is likely to have on Ms. Kinsly's decision making and because of the interplay among the members of the group.

None of these possibilities, however, seems satisfactory as the dominant topic of the case, for each leaves out something important. While the case is definitely concerned with an American urban school, it just as much involves group process. It also includes the relationship between learning and conduct as well as the possible right of parents and others to participate in school governance. Neither the relationship between learning and conduct or the right of parents to school governance is broad enough to include all that is germane to the case. After all, we may be concerned with either of those topics outside the context of urban schools. While group process occupies a major place in the case, it, too, does not embody everything that is important. Even if it were qualified as group process in an American urban school, it still would de-emphasize or regard as incidental what is being discussed, which surely has an important place in the case.

Another possibility for the dominant topic of the case is the difficulty that practical reason faces in trying to improve Rosemont Elementary. That such reasoning is integral to the case arises from two facts. One is that the mission charged to the group by Ms. Kinsly is to help make a decision, specifically, on a response to the scores reported to her by the school district's central office. The other fact is that the committee's discussion is largely devoted to addressing various questions that have to be considered in shaping a response to the scores: the impact of conduct on learning, the importance of interest in learning, the relevance of family background on learning and conduct, the ignorance of Rosemont Elementary's personnel about the family background of the school's students, and the right of parents to participate in school decision making. Determining how to improve Rosemont Elementary confronts enormous difficulty, which arises from various elements in the case. The family background of Rosemont Elementary's students, which lies beyond the control of the school, seriously counteracts the matters over which the school does have control, namely, policies on curriculum, instruction, and discipline. The personnel at Rosemont Elementary lack sufficient understanding of the family situations of their students to know what policy changes are likely to offset unwelcome influences from those backgrounds. There are problems involved in obtaining input from people who are likely to have insights into the backgrounds of the students at Rosemont Elementary. Even if the school obtains input from such people, it has no assurance that it can alter its students significantly. Thus, decisions on how to improve Rosemont Elementary must be regarded as provisional and subject to regular and frequent review.

As the theme of this case, the difficulty of deciding how to improve Rosemont Elementary plainly involves the lesser topics of the urban school in America today, the relation between learning and conduct, and the right of parents to participate in school governance. It also includes group process, albeit not explicitly, for it is the interplay among the members of the group that helps them to identify and try to surmount obstacles lying in the way of their decision making. Seeing no other likely candidates, we will take difficulty of decision making as the theme of the case before us.

THE CHARACTERISTICS OF MORAL AGENCY

Let us now consider the relevance of moral agency to the difficulty of deciding how to improve Rosemont Elementary. To do this, we will start by identifying which features of moral agency are involved in the difficulty.

Freedom

Nobody at the meeting called by Ms. Kinsly asked explicitly about the group's freedom in deciding what should be done about Rosemont Elementary's lack of progress. Moreover, Ms. Kinsly indicated early on that the superintendent's office has left the school much leeway in deciding how to respond to the disappointing evaluation report. Indeed, the group exhibited this liberty when it raised and weighed several alternatives: revising the curriculum further, dealing with class-room conduct, compensating for the educational deficits in the family backgrounds of students, and seeking information on those back-grounds. Freedom, nevertheless, is an implicit concern for the group. When Michelle Isaak asked if the central office wanted the school to change its curriculum again, she implicitly wondered if the group may consider alternatives. When Ernie Girard, Bettye Ervins, and Estelle Gomez discussed the influence of family background on the conduct and learning of the school's students, they implicitly acknowledged the possibility that the students, far from being free, are products of their family environments. Finally, when Ms. Gomez pointed out that school efforts to compensate for educational deficiencies in family backgrounds might be frustrated by those backgrounds, she raised the possibility that the school might have no control over the impact of family background. Thus, the school definitely is free to decide upon curricular and disciplinary measures for improving the school, but it might not be free to counter the factor that most seriously threatens the effectiveness of those measures, namely, the influence of student family backgrounds. That grim possibility, however, is only a possibility, Mr. Girard reminds the group. The school simply will have to see, through trying, if it can modify the family influence.

Knowledge

Two kinds of knowledge involved in the Rosemont Elementary case are professional and nonprofessional. As Ms. Gomez explained the matter, the school's teachers and administrators have been authorized by the public to run the institution because of their professional training and experience. Parents, ministers, social workers, business people, and other "outsiders" presumably do not have the technical knowledge and institutional experience to make and implement school policies. Their knowledge and experience are personal, impressionistic, and at best amaturish. Yet, as Mr. Girard pointed out, the personnel at Rosemont Elementary have a serious cognitive deficiency regardless of their training and experience. They do not know enough about the family backgrounds of their students to be able to determine measures for overcoming the undesirable influences from those backgrounds. The consensual proposal for eliminating this deficiency is to solicit information and suggestions from suitable outsiders. This proposal enables the school's teachers and administrators to retain their professional authority because it ensures that they will be the ones to assess the information and suggestions provided by the outsiders.

There is another kind of knowledge mentioned by Ms. Gomez, namely, that of the consultant, who can provide information and recommendations from the viewpoint of an expert. Because people tend to seek knowledge from consultants with a view to the latter's expertise, they normally defer to that knowledge. They challenge it only when there is something manifestly wrong with it. Nobody at Ms.

Kinsly's meeting, however, suggested that the school should obtain consultants. Why not? It is possible that the group has a bad reason, for instance, the members might feel threatened by an expert. It is possible, on the other hand, that the group has a good reason. For instance, the school might have had an unsatisfactory experience with consultants before; the members of the group might unspokenly presume that there are no experts on the particular student body of concern. Of these possibilities, the last is the strongest reason. But even if there are no experts on the particular student population of Rosemont Elementary, there might be experts on similar populations. If so, these experts might be able to provide information and recommendations quite useful to the school.

Other possible sources of knowledge that Ms. Kinsly's group appears not to have entertained are the information and suggestions that might be provided by other local schools with student bodies similar to that at Rosemont Elementary. Some of those schools might have had some success in counteracting the unwanted family influences on their students. If so, their knowledge might prove useful to Rosemont Elementary. Why the members of the group do not even hint at considering the relevance of knowledge from other schools is not at all clear. One possible reason is interschool rivalry. Another is simple forgetfulness. An additional and far better reason is that the members are confident that no other student body in their district closely resembles theirs.

Purpose and Judgment

Ms. Kinsly's group is assigned a mission early in its meeting: to open a search for a way to improve the academic performance of students at Rosemont Elementary. The group receives this purpose from Ms. Kinsly, and it devotes much of its attention toward fulfilling the mission. To be sure, there are other ends, such as determining how to have effective discipline in the classrooms and how to obtain knowledge about the family background of students. These, however, are raised in connection with what needs to be done to increase academic learning by students. While the members of the group never say that they esteem their mission, they apparently do. All of them have been trying to improve student performance at the school for several years. Also, they accept the mission without hesitation.

But this assigned purpose raises several questions. First, what do the members specifically intend by the academic learning that they want to improve? For them, to be sure, such improvement consists of higher scores on certain tests. What, however, do those tests attempt to measure? Do they try to measure the attainment of important educational features of the students, such as critical thinking, aesthetic understanding, and reading comprehension? Or, do they try to measure something much less significant, for instance, mindless memorization of fragmentary facts and rote learning of isolated skills? Without a clear idea of the academic learning they want students to improve, the members will not be in a position to identify means for leading students to improve such learning. Moreover, the members will not be able to determine when students have attained the learning of concern. Unfortunately, the members of the group, failing to provide a specific statement of this academic learning, might not have a clear conception of this academic learning.

Second, why should improvement in academic learning be a controlling purpose at Rosemont Elementary? It does not follow that a public school has to strive to increase the academic learning of its students just because it is supposed to provide them with an academic education. Ms. Kinsly is probably under pressure from the school district office to improve academic achievement at her school, and the superintendent is probably under pressure from the school board to do the same for the district as a whole. By what principles, however, do any of these parties judge that increased academic performance must deserve immediate attention regardless of conditions at any of the district schools? Are the principles prudential? That is, do Ms. Kinsly, the superintendent, and the board members make increased academic learning their driving purpose because they want to retain or prosper in their positions? Or, do they make it urgent because of another kind of standard, for instance, educational, political, or moral? We do not know anything about the mind of the superintendent or the board members, but we know enough about Ms. Kinsly to believe that career benefit is not all that motivates her. Moreover, we know enough about the other members of her group to believe that they have honorable motives. But we do not know enough about the group's members to identify a norm by which any of them would claim that an increase in academic achievement should have priority at Rosemont Elementary. Nobody at the meeting even alludes to such a norm.

Finally, does not the group tacitly reject its assigned mission and develop a different one for itself? An implicit challenge to the mission begins when the members maintain that classroom discipline has to receive attention before there can be any reasonable hope of increasing academic performance. A new purpose appears when the members agree that their pressing aim is to become informed about the family backgrounds of their students. This shift in priority does not mean that Ms. Kinsly's group does not believe that Rosemont Elementary should attempt to improve the academic learning of its students, but it does mean that the school should not hope to succeed in doing it until later.

That the members of Ms. Kinsly's group challenge the notion that academic learning must have priority at Rosemont Elementary shows that they are reflective, which is a quality of judgment by moral agents. But that they do not state or discuss what they specifically mean by academic improvement at Rosemont Elementary suggests that they lack reflection in their purposefulness.

Deliberativeness

Because Ms. Kinsly's group meets to look for a way to attain a set goal, the group essentially has a deliberative task, that is, one of identifying and weighing alternative courses of action. It identifies several broad alternatives: curriculum revision, greater control of student conduct, and compensation for educational deficits in student family backgrounds. After concluding that the last outweighs the others, the group then rejects its own knowledge of student family backgrounds as insufficient and decides to solicit input from parents and other outsiders. It finally ponders what status that input should have in the policy-making process and what governance mechanism would be appropriate for obtaining the input. In the group's deliberativeness, there are two noteworthy points.

While we recognize that the group has identified and defensibly weighed important courses of action, we also suspect that it ignores one. Specifically, it never entertains the possibility that instructional improvement might help increase academic learning at Rosemont Elementary. We do not know that there are bad teachers at the school, but we do not know either if any teachers are having success with any students from families with deficiencies in educational influence. It is understandable that the members of the group who are teachers might not want to point fingers at their faculty colleagues. But if they do see their collegial relationships as an obstacle, they could recommend that Ms. Kinsly appoint an impartial party to inquire into the possibility of poor teaching as a causal factor. Whether or not the members of the group have good reasons for not even mentioning instruction as a problem is not evident.

The other notable point relates to the right of the group's members to deliberate about policy matters. At the same time that the members of the group legally deliberate about how to improve student performance at their school, most of them do not have a legal right to participate in the discussion; they have only Ms. Kinsly's permission to engage in the discussion. Ms. Gomez's intimation that the teachers at the meeting are legally entitled to help devise policies for student improvement is simply mistaken. It is Ms. Kinsly alone who officially has a right to do this. The three teachers and Mr. Girard are only permitted to help Ms. Kinsly in conceiving a way to better student learning. As principal, Ms. Kinsly has the official right, but not the official duty, to consult with her assistant and faculty. Whether she permits them to consult with her is her official discretion. Moreover, parents and other interested members of Rosemont Elementary's public presently do not have a legal right or duty to participate in making decisions on how to improve student learning or any other school policy. Depending upon the state law governing the district where Rosemont Elementary is located, they might be able to obtain the school board's or the superintendent's permission to help make school policy.

THE NORMS OF MORAL AGENCY

Having identified the features of moral agency as they appear in the Rosemont Elementary case, we now are in a position to examine the case according to the standards of such agency. Let us begin with the freedom involved in the case.

Freedom

We explained that Ms. Kinsly's group definitely has freedom in pursuing its mission, for it is not prevented by external forces from exploring significantly diverse options. From the standpoint of moral agency, this freedom is good and one to which the group has a right. Nevertheless, it is troubling that the group has the freedom only because the superintendent's office cannot think of a promising school improvement policy to impose upon Rosemont Elementary. That office needs to establish deliberative structures and procedures whereby it seeks from the district's schools information and suggestions on program policies that it intends to apply to those schools.

There also is a bothersome aspect of the group's freedom relevant to the choice of its mission. Not only should moral agents have freedom in their deliberations, they also should have it in the choices of their purposes. Initially, Ms. Kinsly's group does not have freedom in choosing its mission, which was assigned to it by Ms. Kinsly. The group eventually does entertain and discuss other possible goals, such as to determine how to improve classroom discipline and how to overcome the educational deficits in student family backgrounds. But it manages this shift in purpose only by dent of its own initiative. If Ms. Kinsly had wanted to, she could have required the other members to stick to the original mission. It will be remembered that she expressed surprise that the group's discussion wound up where it did. Regardless, she needs to recognize the freedom of the other members to help set the group's mission.

Student family background is another area where freedom might be very significant in the Rosemont Elementary case. Because of the strong negative influences of family background, it might be impossible for students at the school to do any better than they now are doing. This means in turn that it might be futile for the school to attempt to improve learning on the part of the students. If the students cannot do any better than they now are doing, they are not accountable for failing to do so, and the school is not accountable for not getting them to do so. While this absence of freedom is a possibility, it is by no means actual, at least, as far as anyone knows. It might be that the adverse impact of family background upon student learning can be alleviated but not by Rosemont Elementary alone. It might take several or more other social agencies working with the school to lessen the influence. In addition, it might be that there are some qualities of student family backgrounds that might support school efforts but have not come to the attention of Ms. Kinsly's group. Either way, the school cannot ascertain that there is a way to overcome the detrimental impact of family background on student learning unless it seeks to understand that background.

Knowledge

The normative knowledge issues in the Rosemont Elementary case bear on the professionalism of the teachers and administrators at the school. Professionals have an authority based upon their expertise, or the technical information, concepts, and skills by which they can provide their respective products and services. For moral agency, the expertise of professionalism poses a question: If people are equal in the respect that they share traits as moral agents, how can a professional person have authority that a nonprofesssional may not have if they both are moral agents? They both value knowledge, have a right to it, and are obligated to seek and promote it. More specifically, is it morally correct for the teachers and administrators at Rosemont Elementary to have the right to help make policy decisions at the school at the same time that parents and other relevant outsiders do not have that right? If the educators and the outsiders are morally equal, do not they both have the same moral rights?

These questions arise only if we assume that moral agents are necessarily equal in specific as well as general aspects. While all moral agents are equal in that they have the same generic characteristics and thus the same generic values, rights, duties, and virtues, they may differ in specific traits. Thus, the physical agility of athletes is different from that of nonathletes; the knowledge of professionals is different from that of nonprofessionals. Because of their expertise, professionals have competencies that are superior to those of nonprofessionals, and in the respect that professionals have superior competencies, they morally have specific rights that nonprofessionals do not have. The surgeon morally has a right to operate whereas a nonprofessional does not. Accordingly, because of their special training and experience, the teachers and administrators at Rosemont Elementary morally may have a right to engage in policy decisions while nonprofessional outsiders morally may not have that right. Hence, the authority that the public has bestowed upon those teachers and administrators to operate the school appears to be morally correct.

Even though school teachers and administrators may have special competencies for operating their institutions, they need not be completely self-sufficient. They might have deficiencies in their knowledge or skills and thus might have to depend upon others for assistance. In the medical field, for instance, general practitioners frequently refer patients to specialists. Hence, once the teachers and administrators at Rosemont Elementary recognize that they have gaps in their understanding of their students' family backgrounds, they morally should seek help to remedy that deficit. Parents and other outsiders with intimate knowledge about those backgrounds are a likely source of help. Consultants with relevant expertise are also such a source as are personnel at other local schools whose students are similar to those at Rosemont Elementary.

Given their failure to improve student performance at Rosemont Elementary, the personnel there would do well to make use of all these sources. If they do, however, they will face a moral difficulty in working with a consultant that they will not face in working with the other sources. The professional training and experience of the teachers and administrators at Rosemont Elementary enable them to understand and assess any information and advice obtained from parents and other outsiders. That training and experience also enable them to understand and assess any information and advice received from teachers and administrators at other local schools. Because, however, the Rosemont teachers and administrators will have a grasp of their students' family backgrounds that will be inferior to that had by a proper consultant, they will not be in a position to fully comprehend and assess the information and recommendations provided by that consultant. Thus, they seem to be in a dilemma. As moral agents, they should act with understanding of their action, but if they cannot comprehend what a consultant reports, they cannot act as moral agents. Is it not immoral, then, for them to act upon what a consultant tells them?

This dilemma, however, is not escape proof. If the teachers and administrators were to act upon a consultant's report without having made any effort to understand it, they surely would be acting immorally. Upon recognizing a lack of understanding of the report, the teachers and administrators morally must try to comprehend it. One step in doing this is to request an explanation from the consultant, who is morally obligated to justify the report. While the explanation may be both written and oral, it also should arise in discussion with the teachers and administrators in response to questions prompted by their lack of understanding. Another step is for the teachers and administrators to discuss the report among themselves. They, thereby, will be able to pool their partial understandings of it but also will be able to help each other see what questions need to be answered by the consultant. An additional step is for them to have the consultant review whatever measures they propose to base upon the report. This step will give them an opportunity to learn what adjustments to the measures need to be made to make their proposals consistent with the report. During their efforts to understand the consultant's report, the teachers and administrators might find good reasons for modifying or rejecting the report, but they also might find good reasons for accepting it.

Purposiveness and Judgment

According to the standards of moral agency, purposiveness is somewhat problematic in the Rosemont Elementary case. Moral agents have to be clear about their purposes; otherwise, they will not be able to assess their ends for what they are and thus will not be able to defend them adequately. But as we have argued, the members of Ms. Kinsly's group, even though they are to consider ways to improve academic achievement at their school, quite possibly do not have a definite idea of the academic learning with which they are concerned. If they do not really have such an idea, they fail the criterion of clarity.

Moreover, moral agents are supposed to choose purposes according to judgments of their moral worth. As we have explained, however, the members of Ms. Kinsly's group appear to accept, at least briefly, the improvement of academic achievement as the urgent end of Rosemont Elementary without having any standards by which to appraise it as such an end. They, therefore, might have failed to assess the suitability of academic improvement as the proximate end of the school. Even when they start giving greater priority to discipline and the understanding of the family background of students, they consider them as goals that are stepping stones to improved academic learning. They seem fixed on the idea that such learning is the central purpose of Rosemont Elementary. Surely, however, there are alternative purposes that might be equally worthy, if not worthier, for the school. Good citizenship and personal development come to mind. The criteria by which the group might deem the improvement of academic learning as the organizing purpose of the school remain dim.

The possibility that the members of Ms. Kinsly's group do not clearly grasp what they mean by academic achievement at Rosemont Elementary suggests, as we have mentioned, that they have not reflected on this matter as moral agents should. If they had, they would have reached, through discussion with one another, a specific statement of the academic achievement they have in mind. They next would have mutually determined if that achievement is positively related to the features of moral agency. If they concluded that it is positively related, they, then, would have judged its worth in developing the students at Rosemont Elementary as moral agents.

To be sure, the group is reflective when it argues that the students, because of their classroom misbehavior, are not presently capable of enhancing their academic learning. Even so, the thoughtfulness here suffers in the respect that it involves the unexamined presumption that improved academic learning should be the ultimate end of Rosemont Elementary and also leads to the rejection of a possible purpose, which is not clearly stated. The group, we should emphasize, does not void the problem of clarity simply by changing missions. When it or its successor starts collecting information and advice on the educational deficiencies of the family backgrounds of their students, it must have in mind the kind of academic learning it wants the Rosemont Elementary's students to attain, for that learning will help define what those educational deficiencies are.

Deliberativeness

There are two kinds of problems involved in the deliberative aspect of the Rosemont Elementary case. One is a failure by Ms. Kinsly's group to entertain a certain course of action. The other is the status of the right of the members of the group to participate in policy decision making at the school.

When deliberating, moral agents are committed to examining alternative courses of action for attaining the end with which they are concerned. Which alternatives they should consider depends partly upon their circumstances and partly upon their talents. The circumstances include resources available to the agents; talents include the agents' knowledge of or ability to learn about those resources and their capability of imagining connections between those resources and the result. As far as we know, the members of Ms. Kinsly's group fail to examine the possibility that improvement in teaching might be needed to bring progress in academic performance at their school. If the teacher members are deterred from pursuing this possibility by their relationships with other teachers, they are capable of suggesting that Ms. Kinsly secure an impartial party to investigate the matter. Intentional silence about the possible need for better teaching might leave a hidden obstacle to whatever solution the group recommends for Rosemont Elementary.

While Ms. Kinsly, the principal of Rosemont Elementary, apparently has the legal right to make policy decisions for the school, the other members of her group do not have that right. They participate in policy making at the school only by the invitation of Ms. Kinsly, who legally may delegate provisional authority. Whether or not we agree with the law, we have to wonder if anyone besides Ms. Kinsly has a moral right to help shape policy at the school. After all, the assistant principal and the teachers there are moral agents, for whom deliberativeness is both a generic feature and a generic right.

To be sure, no person at Rosemont Elementary has a right to engage in policy making just because that person has a generic right to deliberativeness. Otherwise, any moral agent would have a right to help shape policy at the school. Under what conditions, then, would a moral agent be entitled to participate in shaping policies at Rosemont Elementary? There are two conditions. First, the agent is competent to help formulate the goals or means to be embodied in the policies. Second, the agent has a direct moral interest in the entertained policies. More specifically, the policies would directly influence the agent's control over his or her interpersonal actions. According to the first condition, the teachers at Rosemont Elementary probably do not have the right to shape policy on building maintenance, the work schedule of janitors and secretaries, and other support matters. For the same reason, the school's students and their parents are not likely to have a right to help decide curriculum policy at the school. According to the second condition, the janitorial and secretarial staff probably do not have a right to engage in decisions on instructional and curricular matters.

Let us now apply these two criterial conditions to the members of Ms. Kinsly's group. Because all of them seem competent to discuss their mission and deliberate on how to achieve it, they appear to satisfy the first condition. Also, because all of them have a direct moral interest in the policy matters being considered, they satisfy the second condition. But what about the teachers at Rosemont Elementary who are not members of the group? Do not most, if not all, of them satisfy the same conditions? If so, should not they be members of Ms. Kinsly's group? "No," we are inclined to reply. The group would be unwieldly if all teachers were members; also, the members of the group who are teachers may represent the others. This point leads to the question of whether or not Michelle Isaak, Bettye Ervins, and Estelle Gomez represent the other teachers at the school. They seem to in that they appear to be especially concerned with the general learning and conduct situation at the school, not with their particular situations. Even when Ms. Ervins refers to the discipline problems in her own classroom, she is trying to justify her view on a larger point. Nevertheless, we must note that because the teachers in the group were appointed by Ms. Kinsly and not elected by the other teachers, they have not been authorized by the other teachers to speak for them. From Ms. Kinsly's perspective, however, one might allow that the teachers in the group are informed and concerned advisers and that the other teachers may provide input, if they want to, when any proposed policies from the group are placed before them for discussion. There is no indication, however, that Ms. Kinsly will subject the group's proposed policies to review by all other teachers. At most, she explicitly intends to seek further input from some, but not all, other teachers. Apparently, then, Ms. Kinsly should ensure that the other teachers have opportunity for a significant discussion of whatever policy Ms. Kinsly's group proposes.

CONCLUSIONS

According to our analysis of the case, there appears to be nothing profoundly wrong at Rosemont Elementary, but there are various matters that require correction and others that deserve reinforcement. Our specific conclusions will be categorized according to the features of moral agency to which they pertain. Except for one of the conclusions, all of them apply to Ms. Kinsly's group, either collectively or as individual members.

Freedom

1. The superintendent of the district where Rosemont Elementary is located should establish structures and procedures whereby the district's schools may indivually provide information and suggestions on school programs. Without doing this, the superintendent will indefensibly infringe upon the freedom of teachers and school administrators to help shape their respective institutions' programs. The implementation of these structures and procedures need not unjustifiably restrain the superintendent's freedom. Indeed, it might enhance the latter's freedom in that it will help keep the superintendent apprised of obstacles and opportunities at the various schools.

2. Ms. Kinsly should recognize the right of the other members of her group to help set its mission. Instead of initially assigning the group the task of determining a way to improve academic learning at Rosemont Elementary, she might present that task as a possible purpose

but at the same time invite suggestions from the other members about how the school should respond to the central office report on test scores. The group then could choose the best possible task before it.

3. Ms. Kinsly's group should persist in its effort to ensure that teachers and administrators at Rosemont Elementary will gain a firm understanding of the family backgrounds of its students. Through such an understanding, these educators will be able to determine the paramaters of their students' freedom and thus of the freedom that they might have in changing the students' conduct and academic performance.

Knowledge

1. Ms. Kinsly's group is correct in wanting to obtain input from outside parties with intimate knowledge about the family backgrounds of the students at Rosemont Elementary. It knows little about that background and needs to understand it in order to develop strategies for coping with its influence. The group is commended also for recognizing that care must be taken in how information and suggestions are obtained from these outside parties.

2. The group should seek input from consultants who have expertise on the social backgrounds of students similar to those at Rosemont Elementary. If it does obtain the services of such consultants, it should ensure that it fully understands their recommendations and that the programs it proposes are consistent with those recommendations.

3. The group ought to consult with its colleagues at other relevant schools in its district. Their experience might suggest means and obstacles that the group has overlooked.

4. The group has to make sense of the information, suggestions, and recommendations that it obtains from all these sources. It especially has to deal with inconsistencies between the information and suggestions from outsiders and other schools and the information and recommendations from consultants. One way the group might resolve these inconsistencies is to discuss them with the consultants, asking them if their views are defensible despite the inconsistencies or if their views need modification. To facilitate this procedure, the group should obtain the input of outsiders and the other schools before it receives that of experts.

Purpose and Judgment

1. Ms. Kinsly's group needs to clarify what it means by the academic learning that is supposed to be improved at Rosemont Elementary. Once it specifies this learning, it must establish that the district office tests employed to measure such learning are appropriate.

2. The group should articulate criteria for determining the priority of purposes at Rosemont Elementary. If the group wants improvement in academic learning to have priority over all others, it ought to appeal to standards to justify that choice. If it wants the understanding of the family background of students to have priority, it needs to appeal to criteria to justify that choice. If it does not want to give good citizenship high priority, it must have criteria for supporting that choice.

3. As the leader of her group, Ms. Kinsly needs to encourage its other members to be reflective about its mission. She could help do this by suggesting purposes for the group's review rather than assigning them. In addition, she should let the other members know that she is receptive to suggestions from them. If she is under strong pressure from the superintendent's office to pursue a certain goal, she should explain this limiting condition to the group but also invite the members to analyze that goal in terms of its merits as an end for Rosemont Elementary.

Deliberativeness

1. Ms. Kinsly's group should consider instructional quality as a possible causal factor in the lack of improvement in academic learning at Rosemont Elementary. Because it should have entertained this possibility early in its discussion, it now ought to delay making any firm decisions until it has investigated the possibility. If it regards itself as unsuitable for inquiring into the matter, it should secure an impartial party for so doing. If it does determine that poor teaching is a contributing factor, it then needs to inquire how that teaching may be rectified.

2. Ms. Kinsly must ensure that all faculty members at Rosemont Elementary will have an opportunity to review whatever proposals her group makes. She may do this by organizing small discussion groups among the faculty with one of her group's members explaining the proposals to each of the discussion groups. If she does establish these discussion groups, she and the other members of her group subsequently should go over the responses from the faculty and determine

whether or not modifications in the proposals need to be made. She then may present the final draft of the proposal to the faculty to see whether or not it receives the latter's approval. If there are no defensible objections to the proposal, she may proceed with its implementation.

Bibliography

Aristotle (1961). *The Metaphysics.* Translated by H. Tredennick. Cambridge, MA: Harvard University Press.

Barker, S. (1964). *The Philosophy of Mathematics.* Englewood Cliffs, NJ: Prentice-Hall.

Brameld, Theodore (1955). *Philosophies of Education in Cultural Perspective.* New York: Henry Holt and Company.

Broudy, Harry (1979). "Between the Yearbooks." In National Society for the Study of Education, *Philosophy and Education: Eightieth Yearbook, Part I.* Edited by Jonas F. Soltis. Chicago, IL: The University of Chicago Press, pp. 13–35.

Brumbaugh, Robert S., and Nathaniel M. Lawrence (1963). *Philosophers on Education: Six Essays on the Foundations of Western Thought.* Boston: Houghton Mifflin Company.

Descartes, Rene (1955). *Descartes: Selections.* Edited by Ralph M. Eaton. New York: Charles Scribner's Sons.

Dewey, John (1938). *Logic: The Theory of Inquiry.* New York: Henry Holt and Company.

Ennis, Robert H. (1969). *Logic in Teaching.* Englewood Cliffs, NJ: Prentice-Hall.

Etzioni, Amitai (1969). *The Semi-Professions and Their Organization: Teachers, Nurses, Social Workers.* New York: Free Press.

Heidegger, Martin (1949). *Existence and Being.* Translated by R.F.C. Hull and Alan Crick. Chicago: Henry Regnery Company.

Heslep, Robert D. (1989). *Education in Democracy: Education's Moral Role in the Democratic State*. Ames: Iowa State University Press.

——— (1991). "Questions and Erotetic Teaching." *Educational Theory* 41, no. 1, pp. 89–97.

——— (1995). *Moral Education for Americans*. Westport, CT: Praeger.

Hospers, John (1967). *An Introduction to Philosophical Analysis*, 2nd edition. Englewood Cliffs, NJ: Prentice-Hall.

Hullfish, H. Gordon, and Philip G. Smith (1963). *Reflective Thinking: The Method of Education*. New York: Dodd, Mead & Company.

Johnston, Bill J., and Karen S. Wetherill (1995). "Increasing the Relevance of Foundations Study: The Case for Case Analysis." *Educational Foundations* 9, no. 2, pp. 33–49.

Laertius, Diogenes (1925). *Lives of Eminent Philosophers*. 2 vols. Translated by W. D. Hicks. New York: G. W. Putnam's.

Macmillan, C.J.B., and James W. Garrison (1988). *A Logical Theory of Teaching: Erotetics and Intentionality*. Boston: Kluwer Academic Publisher.

Mason, S. F. (1962). *A History of the Sciences*. New York: Collier Books.

McKeon, Richard P. (1951). "Philosophy and Method." *Journal of Philosophy*, 48, no. 2, pp. 353–82.

——— (1957). "General Introduction." In *Selections from Medieval Philosophers*. Edited by Richard P. McKeon. New York: Charles Scribner's Sons, vol. I, pp. ix–xx.

Meyer, Marvin, ed. and trans. (1992). *The Gospel of Thomas: The Hidden Sayings of Jesus*. San Francisco: Harper.

Morris, Van Cleve (1961). *Philosophy and the American School: An Introduction to the Philosophy of Education*. Boston: Houghton Mifflin Company.

National Society for the Study of Education (NSSE) (1942). *Philosophies of Education: Forty-first Yearbook, Part I*. Edited by John S. Brubacher. Chicago: The University of Chicago Press.

——— (1955). *Modern Philosophies and Education*. Edited by John S. Brubacher. Chicago: The University of Chicago Press.

Noddings, Nel (1995). *Philosophy of Education*. Boulder, CO: Westview Press.

Ozmon, Howard, and Samuel Craver (1995). *Philosophical Foundations of Education*, 5th edition. Columbus, OH: Merrill.

Reed, Ronald F., and Tony W. Johnson (1996). *Philosophical Documents in Education*. White Plains, NY: Longman.

Searle, John R. (1995). *The Construction of Social Reality*. New York: The Free Press.

Shulman, Judith H., ed. (1992). *Case Methods in Teacher Education*. New York: Teachers College Press.

Siegel, Harvey (1988). *Educating Reason.* Boston: Routledge.

Simpson, Douglas J., and Michael J. B. Jackson (1984). *The Teacher as Philosopher: A Primer in Philosophy of Education.* New York: Methuen.

Strike, Kenneth A., and Jonas F. Soltis (1985). *Ethics and Teaching.* New York: Teachers College Press.

Sykes, Gary, and Tom Bird (1992). "Teacher Education and the Case Idea." In *Review of Research in Education.* Edited by Gerald Grant. Washington, DC: American Educational Research Association, pp. 457–521.

Index

About the Author

ROBERT D. HESLEP is Professor of Educational Leadership, University of Georgia, and a past president of the Philosophy of Education Society. He is the author of eight books, including *Moral Education for Americans* (Praeger, 1995).

ISBN 0-275-95495-1

HARDCOVER BAR CODE